SOME RURAL QUAKERS
A history of Quakers and Quakerism
at the corners of the four Shires of Oxford,
Warwick, Worcester and Gloucester

by

Jack V. Wood

Foreword by Edward H. Milligan

Illustrations by Mary McColm

William Sessions Limited
York, England

© Jack V. Wood, 1991

ISBN 1 85072 085 1

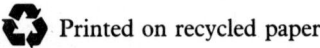 Printed on recycled paper

Printed in 10 on 11 point Plantin Typeface
by William Sessions Limited
The Ebor Press
York, England

Dedicated to Madge Tyson, and the late Charles Tyson, without whose energy and foresight Broad Campden Meeting would not exist.

List of Contents

	PAGE
Foreword (by Edward H. Milligan)	7
Preface and Acknowledgements (by Jack V. Wood)	9
Illustrations of Meeting Houses	
Adderbury (inside the building)	22
Banbury	31
Evesham	41
Sibford	47
Ettington	60
Armscote (from an old steel engraving)	71
Broad Campden	80
Littleton	85
Shipston (inside the building)	101
Fold-out map of our area	Inside back cover
Introduction (definitions and explanations)	
Area covered by the book	12
Quakerism	12
Organisation	13
Spelling and terminology	15
Obsolete words and those with special meanings	15
The value of money	16
CHAPTER 1 THE EARLY YEARS (to 1660)	
Quaker origins and growth	18
Opposition	20
Cromwellian times	21
Blasphemy Act	21
Act of Abjuration	21
Lord's Day Act	22
Vagrancy Act	22
Excommunication	22
Praemunire (Oath of Allegiance)	23

CONTENTS 5

    Republic to Restoration of King Charles II 23
    The nature of surviving records: Incidents in our area 24
        Banbury & district 25
        Evesham 27
        Campden 32
        Warwickshire 33
    Meetings settled 34

CHAPTER 2 THE TESTING YEARS (1661 to 1699)
    Aftermath of Fifth Monarchy Men's Rebellion 35
        Uniformity Act 36
        Quaker Act 36
        Conventicle Acts 36 & 37
        Declaration of Indulgence 37
    King James II, William & Mary and Toleration Act 1689 38
    Incidents in our area 39
        Banbury & district 39
        Evesham & district 40
        Pershore 42
        Campden 43
        Ettington 43
        Other Warwickshire Meetings 44
    Sufferings up to the Toleration Act 1689 45
    Organisation of Meetings and the building of Meeting Houses 46
    Links with America 50
    Viscountess Conway 50
    Death of George Fox 51

CHAPTER 3 THE QUIET YEARS (1700 to about 1860)
    Quakers seen from outside 53
    Changes in Britain: 'Quiet' Friends 53
    Decline and new growth 55
    Sufferings after the Toleration Act 1689 58
    'Is he of good conversation?' 61
        Membership 62
        Marriages 63
        Disownments 64
    Endpiece 67

CHAPTER 4 CHANGING TIMES
    The number of Quakers and attendance at Meetings 68
    The history of Armscote and its General Meeting (1655-1991) 70

Campden becomes Broad Campden (1656-1991) 74
Sibford School 79
East House (sheltered housing) 81

CHAPTER 5   THE EVANGELICAL SURGE 83
The evangelical movement 84
British Schools 84
The adult school, Sunday school and mission movements 85
    Evesham & district 87
    Badsey 89
    Littleton 91
    The Vale of Evesham as a whole 94
    Shipston & district 95
    North Oxfordshire generally 97
    Sibford 97
    Banbury 98
    South Newington, Hook Norton & Adderbury 102
    Note on sources for Chapter 5 103

CHAPTER 6   RETROSPECT
Seed corn 104
From the minutes 107
Bristol Yearly Meeting and its Circular Meeting 110
Visits 111
Testimonies to the lives of those who have died 113

APPENDIX 1   NOTES ON PAST & PRESENT MEETINGS IN OUR AREA 117

APPENDIX 2   HOW FRIENDS EARNED THEIR LIVING 142

APPENDIX 3   BIBLIOGRAPHY & NOTES ON SOURCES 145

SELECTED INDEX 149

Foreword

THIS BOOK MIGHT, I SUPPOSE, have been subtitled 'A religious witness in the south midlands'. It is a record, covering nearly three and a half centuries, of the witness of a Christian body, never very large and at times quite painfully small, in that small tract of land stretching from Banbury and Bicester in the east to Evesham and Pershore in the west, and comprising parts of north Oxfordshire, south Warwickshire, north Gloucestershire and eastern Worcestershire. And if a reader were to say 'What an odd area to have chosen', then the response must be 'Yes, on the face of it, it is: but there are the most excellent reasons for choosing it, which Jack Wood explains in his preface – and I commend the preface to your careful reading as well as the rest of the book'.

Banbury cakes and Pershore plums. The Brown family, at their shop in Parsons Street, certainly produced the former; and there were members of Evesham Meeting who earned their living in the fruit orchards of the Vale. The religious life of Quakers found expression in their daily work. Jack Wood tells us of the Fardons and other Quaker clockmakers of north Oxfordshire and south Warwickshire in the 18th century. In the latter half of the 20th century Peter S. Lamb (1921-1975) of Ettington Meeting brought the same engineering precision to his models, many of which are in the Smithsonian Institution at Washington, D.C. But for the most part the Quaker world of this tract of the south midlands was a world of farmers and woolcombers, of grocers and ironmongers.

A century has passed since Alfred Brown's *Evesham Friends in the olden time* and William White's *Friends in Warwickshire*, and the only local meeting history recently published is Mark Gorman's *Broad Campden Quakers* (1971). Banbury and Sibford, Evesham and Ettington, all have long, honourable, and at times chequered histories which merit detailed study, and it will be one of the triumphs of this book if it inspires others to undertake yet further research into local Quakerism.

The book is, of course, a triumph in its own right and one can but marvel at the way in which Jack Wood has marshalled his material from such diverse sources. We are given information about some 40 local meetings. For the administration of church affairs these were originally grouped not only into five different area Monthly Meetings but into four different county Quarterly Meetings, each no doubt having developed slightly different traditions and procedures. This has meant coping with a mass of material necessarily scattered in different repositories. It has also meant lamenting over material which appears no longer to be extant – as, for example, the minutes of Banbury Monthly Meeting up to 1736.

Alfred Brown and William White wrote in the midst of the adult school and home mission movements of the latter part of last century but, active as they each were in these movements, they were not in a position to record what was going on around them. These movements have (perhaps understandably) been neglected by Quaker historians hitherto and a particularly welcome feature of this book is the attention it gives to adult schools and home missions, and perhaps particularly to the two meetings in the Vale of Evesham – Badsey and Littleton – which sprang directly from the work. There is yet more to be done nationwide on Quaker involvement in home missions and, among much else, we must be grateful to Jack Wood for his pioneering efforts in this field.

It must not be thought that mission effort ('aggressive Christian work' as it used to be described) was confined to the evangelical period of the late 19th century. The travelling ministering Friends of the 18th and early 19th centuries drew vast quantities of 'the world's people' to their specially 'appointed meetings'. And such organised occasions as the Circular Yearly Meeting for the Western Counties demonstrates the considerable background effort – and expense – in organisation as well as the fact that crowds were still drawn by these gatherings. At Evesham in 1771, for example, there were two public meetings on Sunday, two on Monday, and a parting meeting on Tuesday morning – all in a large booth (whose cost Jack Wood tells us) 80 yards long and 70 broad in a field near the town 'which was several times found insufficient to hold the people who flocked thither, and the overflow used to follow such ministers as left the booth, and repaired to the Town Hall, and Friends Meeting House'.

All this effort, in the last resort, depended on the individual faithfulness of countless men and women. The same faithfulness enabled meetings for worship to be kept up week by week, sometimes when conditions seemed unpropitious and discouraging. For Jack Wood's record of nearly three and a half centuries of the witness of this faithfulness we must be profoundly thankful.

EDWARD H. MILLIGAN
January 1991

Preface and Acknowledgements

THE GENESIS OF THIS BOOK was a paper, 'Local Quakers', given to the Campden and District Historical and Archaeological Society in 1987. Banbury and Evesham Monthly Meeting had not long been in existence and I decided that, when I ceased to be its clerk, I would write a history of Quakers and Quakerism in our area, as a contribution to establishing our new identity. Six meetings – Banbury, Broad Campden, Ettington, Evesham, Littleton and Sibford – had come together to form the new Monthly Meeting. They had previously been in four separate Monthly Meetings, but were isolated or distant from others (and Banbury Monthly Meeting was rather small for viability) so they decided, in 1985, to unite in the new grouping. This was the largest reorganisation of Monthly Meetings in Britain since they were set up by George Fox over 300 years ago.

Our Monthly Meeting is at the corners of Gloucestershire, Worcestershire, Warwickshire and Oxfordshire and is mostly rural though we have always been active in the small towns of Banbury and Evesham. The area has never been a main centre of Quakerism and may be typical of rural meetings elsewhere in the country. We think of it as a new grouping but, on going through the archives, I have seen that it has been a Quaker community since the early days and there has been much visiting and inter-marrying.

There are many Quaker records available and it has been necessary to do research at eight record or archive offices. However, there are considerable gaps in the records. The Warwickshire South and Oxfordshire records are fairly good, though there are gaps; the Gloucestershire records seem good but few are relevant to my purpose as only two of our meetings (Broad Campden and Stow) are in that county and most of their records are with Warwickshire South. The Worcestershire records are patchy and a number are lost; for this reason, and others beyond my control, I was not able to do as much research on Worcestershire Meetings as I would have wished.

However, many records were available for examination and there were many books and articles to read. One could do research and follow up minor points for ever; but health, time and commonsense ruled out such extravagance. Some gems have had to be left out, including a minute about a former burial ground used for horticulture; it was reported that 'the only occupant of the burial ground had died'. There are sometimes different versions of the same event and I have had to decide which bits to use; or the story may be tantalisingly short so that one is left in the air and does not know the outcome. For some meetings there is much more material available than for others and this has meant that some get more reported on than others. But, after all, this book is all about nonconformity.

However, one subject on which I have reported fairly fully is the adult school, Sunday school and mission movements which were so important to Friends hereabouts. Though the peak of the work was less than 100 years ago, many of the archives are inadequate and it seemed right to write a fairly wide description. A consequence of this is that readers may find that, in some parts of Chapter 5, there is more detail than holds the interest; I can only suggest that they skip any parts which bore them and forgive my diligence on this part of the book.

The adult school and mission movements were of considerable significance to our forefathers and I hope that, before too long, somebody will feel able to write a history of Quaker involvement in the evangelical movement and the consequences for the Society of Friends in Britain. In fact to do for Britain what Ormerod Grenwood did so well for overseas work in his 'Quaker Encounters'.

I am a very amateur historian, and was past 70 when I started the research, so it seemed best to write a straightforward book and to keep it within bounds; thus I have excluded family relationships together with legal and financial matters. I have concentrated on the 40 or so meetings which are, or have been, within the area and on origins and persecution as well as subsequent events. Those who aspire to write history inevitably 'stand on the shoulders' of those who have gone before; I have found inaccuracies in some of the works of predecessors and this is a comfort to me as I have doubtless made many mistakes myself.

It seemed to me that many people are not just interested in what happened but want to know why it happened; why, for example, persecution was severe, eased and then stopped. So I have included something of my understanding of Quaker history as a general background. And I have tried to make the book intelligible to those not steeped in Quaker history.

Appendix 1 gives notes on all the meetings and meeting houses (including information on where they are) and contains information on matters not in the main text. This may help those who want a quick reference to the main information available about a particular meeting; but other information can be found by consulting the index.

PREFACE AND ACKNOWLEDGEMENTS

Publication of this book was made possible by the generous help of the William A. Cadbury Charitable Trust, the Joseph Rowntree Charitable Trust, the Sessions Book Trust, the Oakdale Trust, the Edith M. Evans Trust and the George Cadbury Fund.

Mary McColm, a local artist of note and a member of Broad Campden Meeting, kindly provided the pen-and-ink drawings and map and thereby brought some distinction to the enterprise.

I started the necessary research without realising the extent of my ignorance of Quaker history. Margaret E. Gayner set me on the right road by advising me how to tackle the records at Bull St. Birmingham; Malcolm Thomas and the staff at the library at Friends House in London continued my education and nothing was too much trouble for them. Edward H. Milligan, in addition to kindly contributing the Foreword, was most helpful in solving problems I raised with him; his knowledge of things Quakerly is phenomenal.

Bryony and Tony Yelloly helped me in various ways; and others helped – by lending or giving me documents or photographs; by recalling past events; by doing some research; and by commenting on drafts and doing proof-reading. The staff of the County Record Offices at Warwick, Gloucester, Worcester, Oxford and Reading steered me through the mysteries of their various index systems and were both helpful and patient.

Without the help of all I have mentioned, this book would never have been published. I am most grateful to them and hope that my efforts have justified theirs.

Chipping Campden   JACK WOOD
Gloucestershire   January 1991

Introduction

Giving Definitions and Explanations

Area covered by the book

'Our area' in this book has been taken as that covered by the meetings set up in the 17th and 18th centuries in the five Monthly Meetings of Warwickshire South, Shipston, Banbury, Campden & Stow, and Evesham; together with a few such as Badsey and Littleton which were established in the last 100 years. Broadly speaking, the area goes from Redditch in the north west to Bicester in the east and Stow-on-the-Wold in the south.

Quakerism

Not everybody into whose hands this book may fall will be familiar with things Quaker and so some explanations seem right. Friends (also called Quakers – the terms are virtually inter-changeable) are members of the Religious Society of Friends and try to follow the guidance of the Holy Spirit in their lives. They do this by seeking the inspiration of the Light of God which is within all of us (the 'Inward Light') and also, collectively, in meetings for worship (worth-ship). They, and non-members known as 'attenders', usually meet in Quaker Meeting Houses which are plain and simple. They meet in silence, seeking to receive the help and guidance of the Holy Spirit in their own hearts or through words which individual Friends may feel called upon to speak ('ministry'). The meeting for worship is central to the lives of Friends.

Friends have no creed, no sacraments, their children are not baptised, they have no consecrated buildings, they do not sing hymns and have no formal prayers. There are no paid clergy; as Friends seek guidance direct from the Holy Spirit they see no necessity for intermediaries. They do not use titles (not even Mr. and Mrs.) and all are deemed equal.

As they seek to respond to that of God within them, and within the meeting for worship, so they try to respond to that of God which they believe is in all men, women and children throughout the world. They testify against all wars and seek to remove their causes. They are much concerned with social justice, with the easing of poverty and with oppression at home and overseas. Not all are interested in theology but all agree with William Penn that 'true godliness dont turn men out of the world but enables them to live better in it and excites their endeavours to mend it'.

Organisation

The word 'meeting' has more than one meaning. It is not, to Friends, just a collection of people who have met together but also a word meaning a body-corporate of Friends who meet for worship or for church affairs. At local levels, meetings were once called 'settled meetings' and later 'particular meetings'; but since 1966 they have been 'recognised meetings'. All local meetings have a meeting for worship (almost always every Sunday) and most also have a business meeting, for church affairs, about once a month. A local meeting for church affairs in time became a 'Preparative Meeting' because a main function was, originally, to prepare answers to searching spiritual questions known as 'queries'. It is still called a Preparative Meeting (PM) though it no longer has set questions to answer. But some local meetings (at one time called 'allowed meetings') did not have their own PM as they were too small, and this function was discharged for them by some larger meeting nearby.

To simplify things, the term 'meeting' is used in this book for all local meetings. The only exception is the mission meeting (together with its variants such as 'gospel meeting', 'prayer meeting' or 'fellowship meeting') which was quite different in that it did not normally include a meeting for worship; this is explained in Chapter 5.

For a district there has been, for well over 300 years, a 'Monthly Meeting' (MM) which oversees a number of local meetings; these meetings send representatives to MM which (usually) meets once a month. The MM is the basic unit of the Society of Friends and, for example, deals with marriages and accepts people into membership. There are today 72 MMs in Britain and they report as necessary to Yearly Meeting (see below).

A 'Quarterly Meeting' (QM) was, until 1966, a body which had oversight of a number of MMs and dealt with Yearly Meeting on their behalf. They were replaced by 'General Meetings' (GM) which, today, cover wide areas and provide forums for discussion and perhaps provide some services; but they are not in the direct line of administration as QMs were. Or a GM can be a body with a special function, such as running Sibford School in our area. In the 17th century the term GM was a rather imprecise one for a meeting for worship for Friends in a fairly wide area but not, usually, for church affairs. And there is also Armscote General Meeting in our area which is different again and thought to be unique in Britain – see Chapter 4. There were, at one time, Circular Meetings; they are described in Chapter 6.

Yearly Meeting (YM) is the national body in London. There are over 60 YMs (or the equivalent) in the world and we in Britain are in London Yearly Meeting. YM meets once a year and, between meetings, its executive functions are discharged by 'Meeting for Sufferings' – a committee set up in 1676. From 1682, YM posed 'queries' on spiritual and day to day matters which meetings had to consider (they also had to answer those from Quarterly Meetings) and much advice was given on how Quakers should govern their lives. There was also a relatively short lived 'Bristol Yearly Meeting' described in Chapter 6.

Naturally, the areas covered by MMs and QMs, and also their titles, changed over the years in accordance with altered circumstances. What happened in our area can be seen from Appendix 1. Throughout the book 'MM' and 'QM' are often referred to without naming which is meant – their titles are often long and reading them would be tedious. If in doubt on which is meant, please refer to Appendix 1.

Every meeting has a 'clerk' for dealing with church affairs: a clerk is both chairman and secretary who seeks to ensure that matters requiring action are considered by the meeting for church affairs – PM, MM or YM as well as other bodies such as Meeting for Sufferings. The clerk tries to judge the sense of the meeting and helps the meeting to reach decisions; and then sees that they are recorded on the spot and that action is taken subsequently. There are also elders and overseers responsible for spiritual and pastoral matters respectively. All posts in meetings can be filled by men or women and all are unpaid. Women now have complete equality with men; but until 100 years ago they had separate meetings for church affairs, though important decisions were taken by men.

There were, until after the 1914-18 war, a number of Friends known as 'ministers' or 'recorded ministers'. In the 17th century they had been known as 'public Friends'. They were men and women (here there was always equality of the sexes) who had a gift for the ministry – that is to say speaking in meeting for worship, which is not the same thing as preaching. Monthly Meetings, in acknowledging that they had this gift, encouraged them to use it, both in their own meetings and more widely. Others wishing to exercise their gifts of ministry (or pastoral care) more widely, laid their concern before their MM and, if it were accepted, they were given a 'travelling minute' and were known as Friends 'travelling in the ministry'.

On their travels, such Friends not only attended meetings for worship and church affairs but also might appoint special meetings to which non-Friends would be invited; and they might visit Friends in their individual families.

Spelling and terminology

Quotations are generally given in modern spelling and some current punctuation has been introduced. Until earlier in this century, Friends did not use the word 'Sunday' but called it 'First Day' and so on for other days in the week; they did not approve, for example, of 'Wednesday' which is named after Wodin. Similarly the months, named after Roman gods and the like, were known by a number, e.g., August was 'eighth month'. (To the uninitiated, phrases such as 'second fourth day in eighth month' may seem a little startling.) For ease of understanding, modern terms are used in this book. And the use of 'thee' and 'thou' for 'you', used by many Friends until well into this century, has not been followed. Such modernisation may reduce the period flavour of old texts but, it is hoped, makes them easier to understand. Some places are today spelt differently (for example, 300 years ago Evesham was 'Evesholme') and such differences are noted in Appendix 1; but modern spelling is used in the text. Up to 1752 Britain used the old Julian Calendar but then changed to the modern Gregorian. The old-style calendar was 11 days behind the new and had the year starting on what is now 25th March. The difference is, for simplicity's sake, ignored in this book and in most cases only the year is given.

In most old meeting houses there are some seats on a bench raised off the floor with an upright partition in front (what the modern furniture trade calls a 'modesty panel'); most are six to eight inches off the ground but some, for example that at Ettington, are higher. They were often facing the entrance to the meeting room and are sometimes called 'ministers' galleries'; all our active meetings have one except the 19th century building at Littleton. They were originally for ministers, elders and overseers and are sometimes divided into three sections. Many old meeting houses have galleries over (usually) the rear seats which were used for various purposes and not just by women. To avoid confusion, an older tradition (vide Hubert Lidbetter) is followed and the former type is called a 'stand' and the latter a 'loft'. Banbury, Broad Campden and the closed meeting house at Adderbury have lofts.

Obsolete words or those with special meanings

'Clear[ness]' means being clear about the rightness of some proposed action.

'Conversation' meant way of life in the 17th and 18th centuries.

'Evil walking' meant following an ungodly life.

'Concern' was, and is, some issue of weight or importance prompted by the Holy Spirit.

'Convince[ment]' means to be persuaded of the rightness of Quaker ways.

'Suffering' referred to imprisonment or violence inflicted as a consequence of following the Quaker way. This included distraint of goods for non-payment of tithes etc.

'Steeplehouse' was the puritan word for a church.

'Professors' meant those professing some faith – usually applied to those in steeplehouses.

'Hireling priests' meant the paid clergy generally.

'Disownment' meant termination of membership by a MM (or QM) for one reason or another. Those disowned could attend meetings for worship but not meetings for church affairs. They could later apply for their membership to be restored.

'Rude' meant violent in the 17th and 18th centuries.

'Mittimus' was, in the 17th century, a warrant for arrest.

'Presented' meant bringing an alleged offender before a court.

'Tithes and church rates.' A tithe was originally the biblical 10% for God and, in the 17th-19th centuries, was statutorily payable to the priest or whoever owned the entitlement. In about 40% of the parishes tithes were 'impropriated' – that is to say the right to receive them had passed to lay owners, mostly the gentry. Church rates were levied in a parish, by a majority vote of those in the parish, and were for the repair of the church, etc. Friends refused to pay tithes or church rates.

A 'tithing' was, even in the 17th century, an obsolescent division of a parish. A 'tithing man' was a petty constable.

The value of money

It is most difficult to indicate the value of incomes in the 17th century. Gregory King estimated, very broadly, the average income of heads of households (including any income from their families) in England and Wales in 1688. With the list of occupations in Appendix 2 of this book in mind, some of King's figures are:–

	£ per annum
Gentleman/Esquire	280 upwards
Clergyman	45-60
Freeholder	50-84
Farmer (which will have included yeoman)	44
Shopkeeper/tradesman	45
Artisan/craftsman	40
Labourer	15

It seems that the majority of Quakers in our area would have come in the last four of these categories; so it will be seen that the fines levied were very considerable in relation to incomes. (*The Economy of England 1450-1750*)

CHAPTER 1

The Early Years (to 1660)

Quaker origins and growth

Quakerism arose in the second half of the 17th century but its roots went deep to (among others) the Lollards of the 14th century. They were hostile to the 'magic' and ceremony of the church and rejected intermediaries between God and man. Baptism was regarded as superfluous because people were blessed by the Holy Spirit and every believer, man or woman, was in effect a priest. By the 17th century Familists had silent meetings, rejected war and advocated a plain life-style. Particular Baptists were opposed to payment of tithes and to 'hireling priests' and had women preachers. Anabaptists refused oaths and rejected war. So various Quaker traits were shared with other early sects – except that no others placed such emphasis on that Quaker essential, the personal guidance of the Holy Spirit.

There were also movements which were political as well as sectarian (in varying degrees) such as the Levellers (who wanted equality for all, land reform and no tithes) and the Fifth Monarchy Men (who forecasted an early second coming of Christ and wanted society drastically reorganised in anticipation of this). These bodies were often confused with Quakers and could be an embarrassment to them.

The Society of Friends had more than one founder but George Fox emerged as the main leader. He was born in 1624 not far from our area, at Fenny Drayton. He was largely self-educated and a healer and visionary. He was powerful in every sense of the word with a tremendous voice and a piercing eye; the force of his personality and conviction can be discerned in his *Journal*. He tried many sects but found none which satisfied him but then, he says, he 'Heard a voice saying "there is one even Christ Jesus that can speak to thy condition" and when I heard it my heart did leap for joy'. He then knew that he could learn from the living Christ within him and did not need any intermediary. An often-used phrase was 'Christ has come to teach his people himself'.

The Quaker attitude was also described as 'primitive Christianity revived' as Friends did not accept many of the doctrines and rituals of the churches which had been established over many years and for which, they maintained, there was no Biblical justification. The emphasis was on the Inward Light which would teach men and women to understand the scriptures and guide them through life. Fox started his mission in the 1640s and, with others, first convinced many in the north of England. Their mission was often called 'The Lamb's war' which was the struggle with no less an aim than the conquering of evil in society.

George Fox and others did not, however, confine their mission to what some might describe as purely religious matters; from the very beginning the Quaker message covered all important aspects of life. George Newman said:

> 'As early in his ministry as 1646, Fox had sought to practise his conception of justice by proclaiming the right of a fair wage and the duty of a day's work for it. He attacked the extravagance of the rich and pleaded for the poor. He understood, as few reformers, the curse of poverty and in 1658 published "A warning to all merchants in London" in respect of their responsibility for it. He protested against the infliction of capital punishment for minor offences . . . [and] against the frivolities and excesses of the time. He was strongly in favour of apprenticeship and vocational education, of the registration of the unemployed and of honest dealing and integrity in trade . . . and, at the root of all his social aspirations, was his love of humanity'.

(George, we have need of thee today!)

From about 1652, 60-70 itinerant Quakers brought their message to the south of England – here we will call them 'Publishers of Truth'. These men and women were constantly on the move and covered great distances; for example, in 1654 (when he first visited Banbury) John Audland was averaging 30 miles a day and visiting perhaps 40 places, passing backwards and forwards through more than 20 counties, all in a matter of a few months. Such travellers were a feature of Friends' work for 300 years and they brought the message to the British Isles and then to the world. The original travellers were mostly young; of those convinced before 1654, the average age was 28 and about one third were women.

The name 'Quaker' originated as a word of abuse. George Fox told magistrates in Derby (in 1650) that they should tremble at the word of the Lord and a magistrate called them 'quakers'. The name came into common usage and Friends accepted it. In the early days Friends called themselves 'Friends of the truth', 'People of God', and 'Children of Light'; the official name, the Religious Society of Friends, was not adopted until late in the 18th century. In his *Journal* George Fox just refers to 'Friends'.

Opposition

Though many thousands were convinced by the Quaker message, there was a strong backlash against them. It was a violent age but the harsh treatment of Quakers was remarked on; Samuel Pepys wrote in his diary 'Indeed the soldiers did treat them roughly and were to blame'. In much of the 17th century, the state and the church were strongly linked and magistrates and clergy tended to act in conjunction. The clergy had their theological grounds for disagreeing with Quakers but their attitude was much influenced by Quakers who:

- called them 'ungodly' and 'hireling priests'. Friends thought that, as Christ had given his message freely and it was still available to those who would listen, nobody should be paid for explaining or disseminating it.
- maintained that church-going was irrelevant because God dwelt in the hearts of men and women. Church buildings were no more holy than other places.
- insisted that tithes and church rates should not be paid. There was no need for church or priests and it was anti-Christian to make such payments.

The magistrates and gentry (which term covered some of the clergy) did not like a number of things such as:

- Friends maintaining that it was right for them to keep their hats on when speaking to social superiors and in court, as it was not right to give 'hat honour' to anybody but God. In the 17th century this was a real insult. Further, the terms 'thee' and 'thou', used by Friends to all men and women, were also regarded as insulting as, generally, such terms were only used when speaking to servants or social inferiors.
- Refusal to swear an oath, which was socially unacceptable and usually illegal.
- Refusal to pay tithes and church rates – which broke the law.

So Friends' actions were seen to be offensive to the 'establishment' and refusal to pay tithes challenged the incomes of both church and some of the gentry. Further, magistrates resented Friends (who were mostly lower class – see Appendix 2) being 'forward' and loquacious. They often condemned to punishment Friends who had annoyed them (e.g., by keeping their hats on) but had broken no law. Magistrates were, to some extent, a law unto themselves and the higher courts were usually reluctant to criticise them. So many Friends suffered unlawfully and, if they put up a good defence, it tended to fall on deaf ears.

In those days a favourite condemnation of those with whom one did not agree was to call them 'fanatics' and it is helpful to try and see 'fanatics' through the eyes of the upper classes. The Civil Wars in Britain had brought much suffering and the many political and religious 'novelties' which had been introduced in and after the Civil Wars had badly shaken the gentry and clergy. Radical political ideas did not come from Friends, who always insisted their message was a Christian one, but their approach was too like that of Levellers and others for them to escape being lumped in with them. The fact that they had such large meetings aroused suspicion that plots were being hatched; and Friends did not go out of their way to calm the fears of the gentry. To quote Barry Reay, 'The fierce enthusiasm and violent language of the early Quakers led many to fear them as a socially subversive phenomenon'.

Cromwellian times

Cromwell, personally, was fairly sympathetic to Friends and on a number of occasions released those wrongly imprisoned; though Friends often taxed his patience. However, the politics of the Commonwealth period brought about the passing of Acts, and the making of Orders, against dissenters.

> *The Blasphemy Act (1650)* was intended to restrain the Ranters and made it an offence to claim to be the equal of God. The Quaker interpretation of the Inward Light could be used in making a charge of blasphemy.
>
> *A Proclamation of 1655* was made to stop people speaking during a church service or 'after the minister had done' – something previously permitted. This certainly applied to Quakers, who often ignored it.
>
> *The Act of Abjuration (1656)* under which people could be required to take an oath denying the authority of the Pope. This was designed to catch Roman Catholics but Quakers were taken in the net because they would not swear an oath.

The Lords Day Act (1656) extended an Order of 1644 and provided for a fine or imprisonment for interrupting the minister in church; required attendance by all at meeting places for Christians (Quaker Meetings were not deemed to be covered by this); and prohibited Sunday travel by all 'vainly and profanely' walking on that day.

The Vagrancy Act of Queen Elizabeth was revised in 1657. The original Act had been designed to deal with 'sturdy beggars' and to have them whipped and sent back to their home villages with a pass to get them there. The revision gave justices a pretty free hand against any thought to be travelling without good cause.

ADDERBURY

Further, Quakers (and others) could be *excommunicated* by a Bishop's court. Thereafter they could be imprisoned by a magistrate for an indefinite period.

Friends would not swear an oath because Christ said 'swear not at all' (Matthew 5.34). Further, they did not accept that there could be two standards of truth, when on oath and when not. If nothing else could be used by a magistrate to imprison a Quaker, he or she could be tendered an oath. This could be done under the Act of Abjuration but a more powerful tool was to require the oath of Allegiance. This oath would be to the King, Parliament, Commonwealth or Republic (depending on who was in control at the time) and, on refusal, the court could send the defendant to prison on a writ of *praemunire*. This could be done under an Act made long before (by Richard II in 1449) and those found guilty were out of the protection of the Government of the day, their goods could be forfeit and they could be imprisoned for as long as the authorities chose. A fierce weapon used against many Quakers.

Republic to Restoration of King Charles II

Oliver Cromwell died in 1658 and in the spring of 1659 Richard Cromwell, who had succeeded his father, was brought down by the army. There were rumours of a new radical religious settlement and other proposals which were anathema to most of the gentry and clergy. An MP said 'Quaker principles and practices are diametrically opposite to magistracy and ministry; such principles as will level the foundations of all government into a bog of confusion'. There was misunderstanding about the difference between Quakers and Roman Catholics. ' . . . and these papists have begotten this present sect of Quakers . . . and so you have here and there a papist working to be the chief speaker amongst them.' George Fox protested against such words, and also against the cry that 'Quakers would kill', but it was hard to stem the tide. There were stories of Quaker witchcraft, child sacrifices and sexual and other immorality. We, today, recognise the extent to which ignorance and deliberate discriminatory propaganda in a time of stress can sour society.

The army tried to run the country but failed; the 'rump' of the Long Parliament was recalled and strengthened and decided on new elections. Quiet steps were taken to neutralise radical and sectarian leaders and, by early 1660, influential people were making overtures to the King in Holland. Harassment of Quakers occurred because many magistrates believed they were plotting against the King. The new Parliament, which met in the spring of 1660, was predominantly in favour of the King and he returned to the throne. Dislike of military rule and of a standing army, fear of what the fanatics and republicans might do, together with dislike of those who advocated non-payment of tithes and other 'levelling measures', had established a majority of the powerful in favour of the monarchy and 'the good old days'.

Before his return to England, the King issued the Declaration of Breda stressing the desirability of religious toleration. However, this was widely seen as a way of letting the Roman Catholics get their rights back and Parliament would have none of it. The King did not press the point but some 700 Quakers were released from prison soon after his return to England. Later, after more Friends had been arrested, the King was petitioned to release them. He was sympathetic, arranged some releases, and proposed a Bill to Parliament which would allow public worship by Quakers and others. However, Parliament did not respond and the rising of the Fifth Monarchy Men, early in 1661, blew away any chance of a new Bill and ushered in a period of renewed and intense persecution.

Rufus M. Jones wrote:

> 'Quakerism began its history with an expectation of growing spiritual conquest. Its first leaders believed they had found, at last, the basis and principle of a universal religion. They thought the propagation of the message as the most normal feature of their lives – the very mission and end of their existence. They were possessed of a great faith, they were filled with enthusiasm, and had a great elan of spirit, which made them almost irresistible among groups of people prepared for their message, while at the same time they were able to stand any amount of opposition and the most stubborn persecution'.

The nature of surviving records: incidents in our area

The information which has come down to us about incidents up to the end of 1660 is mostly about the first visits of Publishers of Truth from the north and the sufferings of those who stood up for their faith. There were many imprisonments but, in this period, fewer cases where goods were distrained. However, we must first look at the nature of the surviving records.

Details of sufferings, given in this chapter and the next, came originally from local meetings in the late 17th and early 18th centuries; this was done as it was thought important that a record be established in London. Much of the information was supplied some years after the event and it appears that some of those working on the compilation were more successful than others in establishing all the facts. Joseph Besse published details of most of the incidents in his *A Collection of the sufferings of the people called Quakers* in the mid-18th century. Though the overall picture he paints is clear enough, some individual cases do raise difficulties. Not only are many descriptions incomplete (was somebody sent to prison held there for 10 days or 10 years?) but it seems that a number of incidents – perhaps many – were not reported at all; and perhaps Besse or his informants were sometimes tempted to exaggerate. However, the story that Besse passes on to us was, in general, incomplete rather than inaccurate.

An example of such difficulties will be found in the case of Robert Field of Ettington (see page 44) who was in prison for not paying tithes. It is said he ran his farm without any assistance even though he was over the age of 90 and unable to walk; and it is remarked (almost in passing) that his two sons were in prison on the very serious matter of a writ of praemunire – but we are given no more information about them. Besse was, in effect, making two separate protests; at the sufferings inflicted illegally and at the state of the English law which authorised brutal treatment. The second applied to all sorts and conditions of men and not just Quakers; but the illegal actions may have hit Quakers much harder than many others. We can understand Friends' reactions to the many savage things done to them and must not let any reservations about some parts of Besse's reports weaken our reaction to what occurred.

As persecution intensified, MMs and QMs took steps to help those in difficulty. Friends were appointed to keep in touch with and help those in prison and their dependants; and to attend court hearings and give what assistance they could. A minute of Oxfordshire QM of 1678 said 'It is ordered that . . . Bray D'Oyly [and others] may take care, as much as they can, to prevent the damage of Friends being presented as popish recusants'. Those involved had visible and tangible support; and the minutes record payments and help to those in difficulty.

Banbury and District

The first reference to Quakers in Banbury was in the autumn of 1654 when John Audland and John Camm visited the town on their way from London to Bristol. They were both Publishers of Truth, the former being a linen draper from Preston Patrick in Cumbria, and the latter a yeoman from the same place. They held meetings at 'the Castle adjoining Banbury' and at Hardwick House in the town. They were supported by Edward Vivers, who was a linen draper and cloth merchant and fairly well-to-do; his father had been a former Mayor of Banbury who had been presented for refusing payments to the church as far back as 1619. Edward soon became a leader of Quakers in the vicinity and was much persecuted – partly, perhaps, because of his standing in the town.

William Simpson, Thomas Marshall, Nathanael Ball and Nathanael Weston were imprisoned and fined in 1655. Friends described their actions as 'Pious zeal and religious declaration of truth at public assemblies in Banbury'. William Simpson was a Publisher of Truth, and a husbandman from Lancashire; we meet him again at Evesham and Campden.

Early in 1656 Ann Audland (wife of John Audland) 'of a comely personage' and Mabel Camm (wife of John Camm) followed their husbands to support Banbury Friends. They spoke in church, were ejected and brought before the Mayor; he dismissed Mabel but sent Ann to prison on a charge of blasphemy (but she may have been released on bail for a period). Jane Waugh (a maidservant of the Camms and another Publisher of Truth from Preston Patrick, who was 'quite illiterate but on fire with the Quaker message') was arrested after preaching against deceit in the market place; Nathanael Weston was arrested after being thrown out of a church as the priest said he could not pray 'with a puritan there'; and Sarah Timms was arrested for telling Lord Saye and Sele 'to fear the Lord'. All three were committed to prison about the same time as Ann Audland.

The four of them came before the Sessions in Oxford in the autumn, when they had already been in prison for up to six months. There were threats that Ann Audland would be burned and a magistrate said he suspected she was a papist. The jury returned a verdict of not guilty of blasphemy but she was found guilty of a misdemeanour through calling a minister a 'false prophet'. She was offered her liberty if she were bound over to good behaviour (i.e. not to do it again) but she refused. She, with Jane Waugh, passed the winter in prison.

> 'In a close nasty place, several steps below the ground, on the side of which was a sort of common sewer that received much of the mud of the town that at times did sorely stink. Besides, frogs and toads did crawl in their room; and no place for a fire. Yet . . . God's presence and peace being with them made the nasty stinking gaol a palace'.

Ann was there for eight months and Jane was there for some shorter period. Nathanael Weston refused the oath of abjuration and was sent back to prison. Sarah Timms enquired how she had broken the law and was told 'sweeping the house and washing the dishes was the first part of the law for her' and she went back to prison for another six months. Richard Farnsworth, a yeoman from Yorkshire and another Publisher of Truth, was present at the trial, supporting the Friends, and later met a justice in the street. On refusing to take his hat off he was sent to prison. He was offered his liberty if he would pay the gaoler's fee; he refused (he had not been charged with anything) and was proffered the oath of abjuration. On his refusal, he was sent to prison and was there eight months, during which time he preached to the people outside through a grating.

William Fiennes, Lord Saye and Sele of Broughton Castle, was an eminent puritan who had been opposed to the execution of King Charles I and who had refused to sit in Cromwell's House of Peers. He attacked Quakers at Broughton, Tadmarton and Banbury. In 1658 he sent Simon Thompson and Nathanael Knowles to gaol for not lifting their hats to him; one was whipped and in prison for 10 months. Simon and some others were sent to gaol by him for having a meeting at Broughton. Simon and another of Lord Saye and Sele's tenants were evicted for no known reason other than that they were Quakers. It is reported that their goods were thrown in the street and that, with their wives and several children, they were there for three weeks in a 'cold wet season'.

In 1659 and 1660 Lord Saye and Sele wrote two anti-Quaker pamphlets *Folly and Madness Manifest* and *The Quaker Reply Manifest to be Railing*; he attacked 'That prating woman Ann Audland who practised not only upon men and women but upon little children, falling down foaming at the mouth, quaking and using unnatural gestures'. In a pamphlet Friends referred to 'The power of God manifest, which caused trembling and quaking, of which we are not ashamed, though thou revile it'.

In the Journals of the House of Lords in 1660 it was reported that 'There are great assemblies of Quakers who meet frequently in great multitudes in the towns of Culworth and Eydon near Banbury, plotting and contriving against the peace of the Church and State' and orders were sent to suppress them. (Culworth and Eydon are a few miles north east of Banbury.) Early in 1660 Edward Vivers, James Wagstaff and five others were gaoled for not paying for repairs to the steeplehouse. Twenty-nine others were taken from a meeting at Banbury and sent to prison for the same reason.

In the late 1650s 'Meetings were settled in Friends' houses, truth prospered and Friends increased' and, by 1660, 40 Quaker households in or near Banbury were contributing to current expenses. In 1657 Friends built a meeting house at the 'backside' of the premises of the 'Flower de Luce' – presumably an inn – owned by James Wagstaff. It was not a permanent structure, and was moved later to the Horsefair site, but it must have been one of the earliest Quaker Meeting Houses in the country; it was certainly the earliest non-conformist building in Banbury.

There was a clear drive by the authorities, after 1655, to stop Friends from outlying villages going to meetings at Banbury. This was attempted by a policy of confiscating their horses by distraint, but does not appear to have been successful.

Evesham

The pattern of events at Evesham was rather different from that at Banbury and persecution was, at times, severe. Two Publishers of Truth went there in 1655; Thomas Goodaire (a yeoman from Yorkshire) and Richard Farnsworth whom we have already encountered. Thomas Goodaire was harshly treated in many places in the midlands and we meet him again at Ettington. However, Humphrey Smith was the most influential of the early Quakers at Evesham. He fought in the Civil War and had been a preacher of note. He came from Herefordshire, suffered for his Quaker faith in Hampshire and Dorset, as well as Evesham, and died in Winchester Gaol in 1663 after a long imprisonment. George Fox said of him 'Through the eternal power of the Lord he was upholden through his sufferings and travelled through many hardships . . . and did convert and turn many to the Lord'.

The first known Friends' Meeting was in Bengeworth, now a part of Evesham, in 1656 in the house of Thomas Cartwright who probably lived in Port St. On a Sunday in summer, the Presbyterian priest brought his congregation (including magistrates) to Bengeworth and incited them against Friends. Humphrey Smith and Thomas Cartwright were arrested and brought before the justices the next day. In court, there was a long theological argument, with priests joining in, and suggestions that the Friends were papists. They were tended the oath of abjuration, sent to prison for refusing to swear it and put in isolation. Robert Martin and other magistrates came to the prison and encouraged the gaolers to maltreat the Friends, but crowds met in the street outside while Humphrey Smith preached to them through a grating.

Several magistrates wanted to deliver the Quakers to a hostile crowd but this was prevented by Edward Pitway. He was a magistrate, and former Mayor, and one who had fought for Parliament in the Civil Wars. The next day Humphrey Smith, and some others, were committed to the main gaol to 'a filthy, dark, close hole' which was open to the air; the populace threw in stones and dirt. Despite this, Humphrey seems to have been able to preach to Friends meeting outside. However, the justices came and imprisoned (in the Town Hall) those who lived in Evesham and put in the stocks those who came from outside the town.

A document of complaint about the treatment was sent to Oliver Cromwell; it was signed by Edward Pitway, Thomas Cartwright and about 50 others – we do not know if all were Friends. For a time there were peaceful meetings outside the prison each day when Humphrey was able to speak. Then Robert Martin again encouraged a crowd to throw 'shovels full' of dirt into the dungeon and this seems to have prevented meetings taking place for a time. Martin also had Quaker books burnt at the market cross. The Mayor sent for all the Quaker prisoners, and also other Friends living in the town, and questioned them about the letter sent to Cromwell. Friends accepted responsibility for it but it was held by the Mayor to be a libel against the justices. As a result, many more Friends were imprisoned until the next Sessions.

The Sessions were in the autumn and a number of Friends were sent to prison, or returned to it, for keeping their hats on. One of them, Thomas

Cartwright, said 'I have lived in swearing, lying, drunkenness and profaneness until now and none of you ever questioned me. But now I have left it, I am punished without cause'. Most were fined and sent to prison, from one Session to another, until they were ready to come to court with their hats off – and no attempt was made to prove anything against them. The Recorder harshly criticised those before him for signing a 'scandalous paper against the magistrates and the town' and many were fined and sent to prison.

Edward Pitway was also before the Sessions as the magistrates had not forgiven him for protecting Friends. He said that he was prepared to prove that the complaint to Cromwell was true – and was fined £20. He was later deposed from the office of magistrate by Edmund Young (now Mayor) and other magistrates. He became a Quaker leader in Evesham.

Edmund Young increased the persecution; he is reported to have said that he would break Friends Meetings 'or else his bones should lie in the dirt'. One Sunday Friends were arrested at a meeting, and also in the street, on the grounds that there were more than eight of them and it was an illegal assembly; 14 were imprisoned and six put in the stocks. Young made a special trap-door for the dungeon and put Friends there without any bedding and refused to allow their dung to be removed. Their books were confiscated and they are said to have been in the dungeon for 14 weeks. A description of their sufferings was written by Humphrey Smith and sent to London for publication. He wrote:

> 'The prison or hole where we are all kept is not twelve foot square and one gaol hole belonging to it four inches wide, wherein we take our food and straw to lie on. And we are forced to burn a candle every day by reason the prison is so dark and so close; and so many in one little room, and so little air, with the stink of our own dung . . . Sometimes, when the days were hot, the breath of some prisoners was almost stopped . . . and when the days were at their coldest, we have no place to make a fire or to walk to keep our bodies warm'.

George Fox visited Evesham towards the end of 1655.

> 'And I heard that at Evesham the magistrates had cast several of my Friends into prison; and they had heard of my coming and they made a pair of stocks a yard and a half high with a trap-door to come to them. I sent for Edward Pitway, a Friend that lived near Evesham . . . and asked him the truth of the thing; and he said it was so. And I went back again with him to Evesham; at night we had a large and precious meeting and Friends and people were refreshed with the word of life and with the power of the Lord. And next morning I got

up and rode to one of the prisons and visited Friends [there] and encouraged them, and then I rode to the other prison, where there were several in prison. And as I was turning away from the prison, and going out of town, I espied the magistrates coming up the town to have seized on me in prison. But the Lord frustrated their intent, that the innocent escaped their snare, and the Lord God's blessed power came over them all. And exceeding rude and envious were the priests and professors about this time in Evesham'.

Shortly afterwards, Margaret Newby and Elizabeth Cowart, from Westmorland, came to visit the prisoners. After a large meeting at Edward Pitway's house they went to the prison. The townspeople were excited against them and, when Margaret began to preach, she was arrested and put in the stocks. In her own words:–

'A Friend did hold me in her arms, the power of the Lord was so strong in me, and I cleared my conscience. And I was moved to sing; and Friends was much broken and the heathen was much astonished. And one of them said that if we were let alone we would destroy the whole town. And the Mayor [Edmund Young] came . . . and took hold of me and Friends did hold me and strove with him, and at length he tore me from them . . . and put both my feet in the same stocks, it being the fifth hour at night, and said we should sit there till the morrow being the market day. And we should be whipped and sent with a pass to our own country. And charged us we should not sing and, if we did, he would put both our hands in also. Nevertheless we did not forbear, both being moved eternally by the Lord to sing in the stocks, each of us with both legs in, and remained until the tenth hour of the next day. And the Mayor . . . sent his officers to fetch us out, the which officers said that these stocks were prepared for George Fox, against he came to the town, and then . . . we were by the officers conveyed away on the backside of the town'.

The Mayor would not allow them to refresh themselves though they were 'much swollen and bruised' and it was a 'cold season' – their hands as well as their feet may have been in the stocks and they had to lie on the ground for 17 hours. Later another woman Friend, Mary Clark from London, came to remonstrate with the Mayor about such treatment; he had her put in the stocks for three hours.

In the spring of 1656 (five months after the letter was sent to Cromwell with all or most of those concerned still being in prison) a reply was received through Major-General Berry. Berry summoned the Evesham Magistrates to see him at Worcester and told them that Friends were peaceable people

THE EARLY YEARS

BANBURY

and must be protected in their religion. He also told Friends not to disturb churches. The Friends in prison were released on his orders but, a few months later, several had goods distrained to a greater value than any fines imposed. However, Cromwell heard of this and ordered that the goods be returned.

Until Friends had their own meeting house in Cowl Street (in 1676), they met in private houses, mostly those of Edward Pitway, Thomas Cartwright, Thomas Hyatt and John Washbourne. Persecution seems to have been intermittent in the latter half of the 1650s. Friends were prosecuted for non-payment of 'steeplehouse rates' and goods were taken from them beyond the value of that legally demanded. William Simpson was sent out of town for 'exhorting the people in the streets of Evesham to repent and fear the Lord'; and Thomas Woodrove was in prison for three months for a similar reason. Others were imprisoned for being at a meeting, or having hats on in court or 'speaking to a priest'.

George Fox visited Evesham again in 1656 (he had had a savage imprisonment in Launceston since his last visit) together with John Camm.

John was in failing health and died soon afterwards. George Whitehouse and William Dewsbury (Publishers of Truth from the north) were in Evesham in 1657. It was clearly felt that Evesham Friends needed support.

Early in 1660, when the country was somewhat disturbed, another big effort was made to destroy Evesham Friends. It started quietly with three Friends (one was Edward Pitway) being arrested and sent to prison for refusing to swear. Next day 20 Friends were taken from their meeting and imprisoned. A few days later 45 Friends (34 were women) were imprisoned. In the next week 15 more were taken including 13 women. So 83 Friends – 47 being women – were imprisoned in less than a fortnight; an indication of jumpiness of officials in those troubled times as well as the number of Friends then in Evesham.

Two of the Evesham Magistrates, Robert Martin and Edmund Young, were particularly violent and oppressive and 'whooped up' the crowds against Quakers. It seems (though is not fully proven) that Young's widow, Elizabeth, later gave some land to Friends for the meeting house they were to build; this may have been an act of reparation. It is not possible to say where the prisons (apart from the Town Hall) which held Friends are, but there is a tradition that one of the places is the basement of an old black and white half-timbered dwelling house on the right as one goes from the market place towards the church gates. It is also said that Friends were held in what is now the Almonry Museum.

Campden

In 1657 William Simpson came into Campden with John North and Thomas Kite and went to the parish church on a Sunday. They waited until the priest had done but as there 'was to be a sacrament, as they call it', Simpson proposed to speak to the people 'in the high place'. There was a demand for him to be taken away and a crowd 'being filled with envy ran violently upon him and dragged him out of the steeplehouse'. The doors being closed William Simpson remained in the graveyard; he later called upon the priest to allow him to speak and, in consequence, was 'dragged about the yard'. The next Sunday he was there again and this time was sent to prison. The warrant for his arrest called him a 'sturdy beggar' and said he had a 'low forehead, brown hair and was about thirty years of age'. Simpson said he was no vagrant, 'had not begged neither was he wandering, no more than in the service of the Lord who moved him from city to city and country to country'. The constable took him many miles away but he was back in Campden later. He was right in saying that he travelled a lot, he was not only in trouble with the authorities in Campden, Evesham and Banbury but he was active at places outside our area.

Also in 1657:
'William Webb of Broadway, while passing through Chipping Campden towards a meeting, was observed by a justice who demanded ten shillings of him for travelling on a Sunday; and for non-payment ordered him to be set in the stocks. The same justice caused the like punishment to be inflicted on William Russel, Mary Drury, Alice Butcher, Joanne Wigan and Thomas Lane for going to a meeting at Broad Campden – the parish where they dwelt'.

Late in 1660,
'Being the fifth day of the week, we the people of the Lord called Quakers, in and about Broad Campden in the county of Gloucester, being there peaceably met together in our hired house to wait upon the Lord to worship Him in spirit and in truth. Soldiers, one of them being so drunken it was hard for him to get on his horse, came in amongst us with their warlike weapons and said they must disturb us; forthwith thrust us out of our house both men and women. And, being encouraged by drunken men, drove us from town to town (threatening to fire their pistols) and delivered us to the tithing men (so called) wherein they kept us prisoners without any order they would show us, though we oft demanded it. And on the morrow had us before one Thomas Overbury, in commission to do justice, who demanded of us the oath of Allegiance. But for conscience sake we would not swear and breach the command of Christ who hath said in the Holy Scriptures 'swear not at all'. He moderately confessed we ought not to swear if it were a matter of conscience to us or believed it to be evil. But he said he was sworn to execute the law and so committed Henry Duffie, William Russel, Thomas Cale, Edward Warner, Thomas Moseley, Thomas Keith and William Keite to the common gaol at Gloucester, where the felons and other prisoners abused them taking away their hats and coats'.

Warwickshire

In the summer of 1660, John Carkitt, Edward Carkitt and Edward Walker were taken from their work in harvest at the suit of William Bishop of Over-Brailes, an impropriator of tithes (i.e. not clergy), and committed to the county gaol at Warwick, where they were kept the first two nights in a dungeon 20 steps underground. A few days later, George Wyatt of Brailes was sent to Warwick for the same reason. (Today, Warwick Castle is open to the public. There is a 'Dungeon and Torture Chamber' which can be visited. It is 21 steps down from the castle bailey.)

Towards the end of 1660 Humphrey Becland, Richard Woodward and John Tombs were taken from the meeting at Alcester 'and carried before Justice Lee who abused them by both words and blows and, not permitting them to speak in their defence, committed them to prison where the gaoler put them in irons and shut them up in the dungeon amongst the felons. Thus they were kept close prisoners, from one Assize to another, and never brought to any legal trial'.

Meetings settled

In 1656 George Fox held a meeting at Edge Hill near Radway in Warwickshire.

'And I had a meeting at Edge Hill which was very rude for there came there Ranters, Baptists and several sorts of rude people; for I had sent word to have a meeting there a matter of three weeks before. And I went up to it, where there were many people gathered to it and many Friends and people came from far to it . . . And many were turned to the Lord Jesus Christ by his power and spirit . . . All was quiet and peaceable and passed away quiet so that the people said it was a mighty powerful meeting and the presence of the Lord God was felt by his power and spirit amongst them'.

The meetings in our area in that year (with the dates of their first known year of meeting in brackets) are thought to have been:–

Banbury (1654)
Armscote (1655)
Shipston (1655)
Adderbury (1656)
Campden (1656)
Evesham (1656)

Local meetings which came into existence in the next seven years were:–

Brailes (1657)
Radway (1659)
Alcester (1660)
Ettington (1660)
Redditch (1660?)
Long Compton (1661)
Broadway (1662)
Pershore (1662)
South Newington (1663)

CHAPTER 2

The Testing Years (1661 to 1699)

Aftermath of the Fifth Monarchy Men's Rebellion

The Fifth Monarchy Men rose in rebellion in London at the beginning of 1661. They believed that Christ's second coming was about to take place and that urgent and drastic remodelling of society was essential. George Fox recorded in his *Journal*:

'... and then the Fifth Monarchy Men rose and a matter of thirty of them made an insurrection in London ... at midnight ... the drums beat and they cried "Arms, arms" which caused the trained bands and soldiers to arise both in the city and in the country ... In the morning ... all the city and suburbs were up in arms and exceeding rude; all people were against us and they cried "There is a Quaker's house, pluck it down" ... and it was hard for any sober person to stir for several weeks time'.

A Proclamation was issued prohibiting meetings of Anabaptists, Fifth Monarchy Men and Quakers, and the justices were ordered to tend the oath of Allegiance to those found at meetings. Quakers took the main force of the backlash and some 4,230 (almost all men) were imprisoned (of which 240 were in Warwickshire). The Fifth Monarchy Men, before they were hanged, said that Quakers had had no part in the rising; and many Quakers were released in the next few months.

Friends tried hard to convince the Government that they had had no connection with the Fifth Monarchy Men, had no political aims and (though dissenting in matters of religion) were peaceful and loyal subjects. In 1661 George Fox and others sent a long declaration to the King (*By the harmless and innocent people of God called the Quakers*) within which was what has become to be known as the Friends' Peace Testimony. Others made protests too; for example in a letter of 1660, sent to the King, Margaret Fell wrote (with Fox's approval):

'We are a people that follow after those things that make for peace, love and unity; and it is our desire that others' feet may walk in the same . . . We do deny and bear our testimony against all strife, wars contentions . . . treasons, treachery; and false dealing we do utterly deny . . . and speak the truth in plainness and singleness of heart'.

Margaret Fell was often called 'the Mother of Quakerism' and later, after the death of her husband, she married George Fox.

A period of renewed persecution was to follow but, throughout, Friends continued to proclaim their faith publicly and did not 'go underground'. They worshipped in their meetings, openly and without pretence, even when it became illegal to do so. If a meeting house was occupied or destroyed, then they met in the street. If the leaders were put in prison the rest carried on. If more were arrested, the meeting might be reduced to women and children; but they carried on. Those not in prison often held their meetings in the street outside the prison. In fact they refused, publicly, to refrain from doing what they considered to be right. John Noakes, speaking of Worcestershire, said:

'Presbyterians occasionally attended church services to avoid penalties but other non-conformists refused. The Quakers were remarkably firm in their opposition never visiting the sacred edifice except for the purpose of bearding the parson and challenging his disputation'.

Within a few weeks of the Fifth Monarchy Rebellion, Parliament started on their first legislative attack which built up to the *Uniformity Act 1662* and the *Quaker Act 1662*. The former imposed the Anglican Prayer Book on all. The latter provided for action against those refusing an oath; against those maintaining that it was morally wrong to take an oath; and against those leaving their homes and attending meetings of more than four people over the age of 16. Fines were to be levied and, on third conviction, transportation beyond the seas was to be carried out. Many Friends suffered under these Acts (it is estimated that 1,300 were in prison in 1662 after the Quaker Act) but, where transportation seemed likely, it was often hard to get a jury to convict – and also hard to get sailors prepared to take any convicted away by sea. Friends were under much pressure in the second half of 1662 and in 1663. The King ordered the release of Quaker leaders but, this having been done, their places in prison were soon taken on the arrest of other Quakers.

The Conventicle Act 1664 came in the wake of a northern plot against the King; Friends were not involved but were commonly thought to have been. It aimed to prevent conventicles (e.g. Friends' Meetings) and worship other than with the Anglican Prayer Book. Again, there was provision for fines and imprisonment. Refusal to take an oath meant that a conviction was recorded; and transportation beyond the seas was to be paid for out of the offender's lands and goods. Justices, acting without a jury, could convict and pressure was put on local officials to carry out the provisions of this Act. Quakers were almost the only dissenters penalised and it was said that, by the end of 1664, every Quaker leader had been in prison as a result of this Act and that, in some places, every Quaker had been confined. But it must also be said that then, and in the coming years, some magistrates exercised their humanity and commonsense in making judgements.

After a lull there came the *Conventicle Act 1670* which was even harsher than the previous Act and referred to conventicles as 'rendezvous of rebellion'. It could be enforced by only one justice acting without a jury. Transportation was dropped as a penalty and, instead, heavy fines were to be applied; the intention was to ruin people financially. The justices could break into suspected houses and use the militia to disperse or prevent meetings. Local officials who did not implement the Act could be fined; the justices themselves could be fined £100. Half of any fine could go to any informer and the consequence was that a rash of informers emerged throughout the country. Andrew Marvell described the Act as the 'quintessence of arbitrary malice'.

On the eve of a war with the Dutch, the King issued the *Declaration of Indulgence 1672* which, in effect, suspended the penal laws and permitted meetings; this was not, perhaps, for the love of dissenters but was aimed at keeping the 'home front' quiet during the war. Friends sent the King a list of those whom they thought should be released from prison; 491 were released, including 125 held on a writ of praemunire. Parliament did not challenge the act of clemency but did contest the King's right to suspend the penal laws. The King, under pressure, cancelled the Declaration of Indulgence in the following year; but those released from prison remained at liberty. In fact there was a breathing space, and less persecution, for a year or two.

The King, again in difficulties and wishing to placate the Anglican Church, took new measures. These were the *Orders in Council 1675 & 1676* which provided for a fine of £20 for each month an adult did not attend the Anglican Church, and which also ordered more diligent application of the penal laws. From now, and until his death in 1685, Friends got little help from the King and, in 1676, set up the Meeting for Sufferings in London which arranged support for those in difficulties with the law. In 1678 Titus Oates and others stirred the pot with their rather wild accusations of plots against the King, who again called for action against dissenters. In 1680 the

House of Commons started work on a Bill to ease the lot of dissenters but the King dissolved Parliament before it could be fully discussed. The King was now (secretly) subsidised by French money and ruled without Parliament until his death. But he still needed the support of the Anglican Church who asked for, and got, continuing pressure on Friends and others; about 1,000 Friends were in prison in 1683.

King James II, William and Mary and the Toleration Act 1689

Charles II died in 1685 and was succeeded by his brother as James II. The Quaker William Penn persuaded the new King to reduce the pressure on dissenters, and this was done by issuing a general pardon and suppressing the numerous informers; and many Quakers were released. James II, who was a Roman Catholic, wanted to remove the restrictions on his co-religionists, and issued a Declaration of Tolerance in 1687; however, it had no statutory force as it had not been approved by Parliament. Opposition to him greatly increased and when his (Roman Catholic) wife gave birth to a son the Protestant leaders foresaw a line of Catholic Kings succeeding him. They opened negotiations with William of Orange who was James's son-in-law (he had married Mary, a Protestant daughter of James's first marriage). William and Mary were invited to take over the throne and rule jointly – which they did in 1688, King James retiring to France. The new King was styled William III.

One of the first Acts of William and Mary's reign was the *Toleration Act of 1689* which gave freedom of worship to dissenters provided they registered their place of worship; and it became illegal to enter a place of worship for the purpose of disturbing those present. So, quite suddenly, toleration was granted after years of persecution. William was in favour of toleration but, more to the point, so were those who had invited William and Mary to the throne. The gentry regarded themselves as the 'natural leaders' under the King having held that role for hundreds of years. In their view, the ordinary man (and even more the ordinary woman) had no place in politics or the running of the nation. They were especially against what they called 'mechanic preachers' such as John Bunyan and George Fox. However, many had come to recognise the futility of persecution; legal and financial penalties were clearly not going to destroy dissent, particularly Quaker dissent, and it came to be accepted that uniformity in religion was no longer possible.

The uncompromising actions of Friends, over a period of some 40 years, was an early example of what can be achieved by non-violence; but the toll had been heavy. Tithes and church rates remained a problem, with much suffering by distraint of goods, for nearly another 200 years. An Act allowing affirmation, instead of swearing oaths was passed in 1695; Friends were not happy about its wording but a more satisfactory one was passed in 1722. A remaining problem was the legislative and other actions which prevented Friends (and other dissenters) from being MP's, going to a university or holding public office.

Incidents in our area

The period 1661-1689 was a period of considerable persecution and Friends had to devote much of their energies to sheer survival. Despite this, matters such as the settling of new meetings, building an organisation, providing for women's meetings, building new meeting houses and developing the Quaker way of life were not neglected. A report made at that time sets the scene on persecution; it was said that, in 1662, Friends from every meeting in Warwickshire (from outside as well as within our area) were in prison and that, in many cases, all the men in a meeting were in prison.

Banbury and district

In August 1661 a party of soldiers entered a meeting at Banbury and 'barbarously abused those who were there, beating and bruising many'. They dragged them out of the meeting house and continued to beat and misuse them. Two were arrested; one was Jane Waugh whom we met in the last chapter. Late in 1661, the Lords of the King's Council asked the Lord Lieutenant of Oxfordshire 'To prevent and dissipate all conventicles of sectaries and like dangerous people' and especially 'A numerous conventicle of insolent fanatics who usually assemble in the town of Banbury and refuse to disperse themselves but obstinately continue their meetings'.

At the end of 1663 soldiers again came to Banbury Meeting. They took the names of those present including Henry Philips. Later, he was called before the justices who demanded sureties for good behaviour and an undertaking that he would not go to meetings again. He refused, and was sent to Oxford gaol until the next Quarter Sessions where he was tendered the oath of Allegiance – and again at the next two Sessions. He continued to refuse and was declared to be under writ of praemunire – and was in prison for eight and a half years. Similar treatment was given to James Wagstaff and two others arrested while on business at Warwick; they too were sentenced under a writ of praemunire and were in prison for over eight years.

In 1662 Edward Vivers and 13 others were fined for holding meetings at Milcombe and Banbury, and others were imprisoned for refusing the oath of Allegiance. In 1664 Banbury Friends were shut out of their meeting and met in the street outside. Richard Vivers was speaking when the Mayor came past – who fined him £20 and a further £15 by distress; and there were other incidents.

In 1665 the meeting house, which had earlier been at James Wagstaff's premises, was taken down and re-erected on the present site in Horsefair. Later Edward Vivers was arrested by an order of the Lord Chancellor (and Lord Lieutenant of Oxfordshire), Lord Clarendon, and sent to prison at Oxford. He appeared before the Assizes or Quarter Sessions at Oxford several times but nothing was brought against him and he was recommitted each time. Eventually, James Fiennes, Lord Saye and Sele (who had recently succeeded to the title) became Lord Lieutenant for Oxfordshire and had Vivers before him. The only cause which could be shown as justifying his commitment was that he had built a meeting house and 'caused a burial ground to be walled around'. He had then been in prison for two and a half years and was set at liberty. It has been suggested that Edward Vivers paid for the land at the Horsefair Meeting House but this is not certain.

Other incidents were at Shutford, South Newington, North Newington, Hook Norton and Milcombe in particular. Imprisonment (up to a year) or fines (or both) were inflicted; and a Friend at Milcombe was fined the very large sum of £100. A Shutford Friend had goods distrained because, when called as a Juryman, he refused to swear the oath. Two from Hook Norton died in prison at Oxford. A Banbury Quaker, present at the burial of a Friend, spoke and exhorted those present to 'remember their latter end'. A justice, who was also present, fined him £20; and a further £22 worth of goods was taken by distraint. When the officials seized his goods, they ordered some present to help them carry them away; on refusal one was committed to prison by a constable and another was threatened with the stocks. Two Sibford Friends, arrested at a meeting at Banbury, were charged with behaving 'in a riotous and tumultuous manner with force of arms' – which seems an excessive charge for pacifists.

Evesham and district

Early in 1661, a constable came to the meeting at Evesham and hauled all the men out; 30 were kept in the Town Hall overnight. Next morning they came before a justice who sent 19 to prison. Early the next year others were sent to prison for 'Having assembled themselves under the pretext of joining in religious worship, to the great endangering of the public peace and safety and to the terror of the people'.

EVESHAM

In 1662, a Lieutenant with a party of the trained bands came to Broadway Meeting 'and commanded those who were met there to depart'. One of them, Robert Bayliss, did not move quickly enough and the Lieutenant suddenly drew his sword. 'This so terrified Bayliss's wife (who was nearing her confinement) that she was in great danger of her life.' Later that year, Major Wilde (we meet him again below and he was active against Friends outside our area) came with a party of soldiers to Evesham Meeting and arrested several Evesham and Broadway Friends there. He bailed them to appear at Worcester the next day, with the exception of Richard Walker who was

> 'Over 60 years of age and sick, yet he was driven before the horses on foot and, when not able to keep pace with them, was dragged along and threatened with a pistol. At length they set him upon a horse, whipping it hard so that Richard was in great pain. He asked for mercy but only got derision. Eventually he reached the prison at Worcester; but his hardship so weakened him that he died shortly after commitment'.

There were other sufferings in and around Evesham but, after 1660, persecution was less than in the years before. At Banbury and other meetings the position was reversed. It may be that some of the persecution was instigated by individuals or groups and, as circumstances changed, so did the onset of persecution.

Pershore

In 1662 (the first date we have for a meeting there) the meeting at Pershore was broken up by a party of soldiers. With drawn swords they forced Friends along the street, beating some of them. They were brought to the gaol at Worcester and confined there, though no mittimus was ever issued and they were not examined by magistrates. George Fox was there in 1667:

> 'We had many meetings up and down that country [Worcestershire] amongst Friends [and] we had a general men's meeting at Pershore at Henry Gibbs' house, where we settled all the meetings in Gospel order. And the Sessions being in town that day, Friends were very much concerned lest they should send some officers to break up our meeting; but the Lord's power chained them all so that our meeting was quiet. And after I was out of town there was one Major Wilde, a wicked persecuting man, and some of his soldiers enquired after me; but I had passed away to Droitwich and left Friends settled in good order'.

Campden

In the summer of 1682 Richard Parsons (Chancellor of Gloucester) went to the meeting house at Campden at a time when nobody was there. 'He, with such as attended him, burst open the doors and broke the windows all to pieces; and departed with many threats.' Shortly afterwards he received information about the meeting there and issued some warrants. As a consequence, various goods were taken from Friends by distraint. From William Heyders of Stanway goods and timber worth £30; from Gervas Harris of Willersey livestock worth £20 and from Paul Heron a cow worth £3. Further action was taken for absence from the church; goods were distrained from three Friends, and Gervas Harris was committed to prison. There is in existence at Gloucester Record Office a paper which records the payment to the Sheriffs of £5 from 'Richard Parsons B.A. one of His Majesty's Justices of the Peace . . . being His Majesty's share of moneys levied upon several persons at Broad Campden upon the act of suppressing seditious conventicles'. It would seem the King only got £5 out of something over £50 taken; so some informer – or perhaps Parsons himself – did quite well out of it.

In 1685 Charles Allen of Pebworth had livestock taken by distraint.

'A servant of Charles Allen, standing by, but not being a Friend, seeing this [i.e. the distraint of goods] thought it good to secure some money of his own. Seeing about six shillings in a pair of breeches hanging up he took it. The gaoler demanded the money which he refused to let them have. They threatened to shoot him so he was forced to give it up.'

Ettington

Ettington was a small meeting but had much persecution after the Restoration. In 1661 eleven Friends were taken from their homes, or from their employment, or from an inn where they were giving thanks before supper; this last was regarded as 'preaching at a conventicle'. They were all sent to prison and brought before a justice who tendered them the oath of Allegiance. On refusal to swear they were sent to prison under a writ of praemunire and lay there for over 10 years.

We encountered Thomas Goodaire at Evesham and now meet him again in 1661.

'Thomas Goodaire, preaching in a meeting at Ettington, was taken before one of the Deputy-Lieutenants who tendered him the oath of Allegiance and, for refusing to swear, sent him to Warwick gaol; and with him one Thomas Cooke who, in love to Goodaire, accompanied him from the meeting to see the issue. At the next Quarter Sessions the oath was again tendered to them and they were sent back to prison under sentence of praemunire, though never legally convicted by any jury. When they had been long in prison they represented to some of the persecuting justices the hardship of their case and that there was "A just Judge in heaven who beheld their innocent cause". To this they received the profane answer "We shall exercise the power we have on earth against you and, when you shall come to heaven, you may take your turn to exercise your power there". They continued in prison for 13 years.'

Also in 1661, Dorothy Lewis, a widow of Upper Ettington aged 'three score years and upwards', was taken to prison for non-payment of tithes and was there for six months. She was also distrained for £45 worth of goods when the tithe due was only £8. One of her sons was later imprisoned for eight months and, in the following year, the goods of another son were seized, to the value of £18, when only £8 was due. And in 1664, and again in 1665, Dorothy had livestock seized.

In 1662, Robert Field of Upper Ettington 'above 90 years of age' was arrested for non-payment of tithes. He was unable to walk and was drawn on a dung cart to Warwick gaol. While in prison, corn in the field and two horses were seized. His troubles were compounded by the fact that his sons were in prison under a writ of praemunire and he had no servants or assistant. Five years later (he was then described as '93 years and upwards') he had a brass pot taken from him to the value of £8 for not going to a steeplehouse a mile away, though it was known he was so infirm that he could not leave the house. In 1663 Richard Lucas of Ettington, for 6d demanded in tithes, was prosecuted in the Ecclesiastical Court, excommunicated and committed to Warwick gaol where he was a prisoner for many years.

In 1670 meetings were being held in the house of Samuel Lucas of Ettington. The priest of the parish 'Pretended himself to be bound in conscience to oppose and accordingly he became an informer telling them that he was obliged, in a point of conscience, to prosecute the law against them'. He brought an officer to the meeting and took the names of those present – and Samuel Lucas was fined £40. Later he informed again, and Samuel Lucas was fined £10; and others were fined and had goods taken under distress.

Other Warwickshire Meetings

In 1661 at Long Compton,

'Friends being peaceably met together in the fear of the Lord to wait upon him. There came in men with swords and pistols swearing many bitter oaths that they would pistol Friends and run them through. And with violence broke up the meeting, hauling out the women, searching their pockets and cutting off their [illegible] and keeping the men within the house . . . and taking away their knives and other necessities but [found] no carnal weapon to hold against any. And after a while they had them forth out of the house, pushing some and striking others, and so driving them to what they call their church and kept them in prison that night. And on the morrow, with armed men guarding them, to Warwick and there kept them in prison for two days before examination and being brought before the commissioners. And they tender them the oath of Allegiance and because they, for conscience sake would not swear, they commanded them to prison'.

Much the same happened about that time at Radway, where Friends were in 'a dark hole of the dungeon the place being very little, and Friends so many, that they could not lie down. The place being very low and very close and they being constrained to ease their bodies in the same place it caused the room to be very noysome'. One of them, Stephen Potter, being extremely weak, his wife, 'a poor lame woman', came with his sister to visit him; on which they were sent to Bridewell and whipped.

In 1661 two Shipston Friends were taken by soldiers while on the highway and taken before magistrates, who accepted that they had been arrested illegally but, nevertheless, tendered them the oath. On refusal they were committed to prison as 'disturbers of the realm' and the gaoler was instructed not to let them confer with anybody save in his presence. In the 1660s and 1670s a number of Shipston (or Armscote) Friends were imprisoned or fined for non-payment of tithes or not going to church. Those imprisoned were there for varying periods; one, who was excommunicated, was in prison for eight years until released under the King's pardon in 1672.

Sufferings up to the Toleration Act 1689

It is hard to quantify sufferings. The instances given in this book are a number of local 'snapshots' and there were other incidents. William C. Braithwaite thought it likely that the number of Friends in Britain who suffered from imprisonment, or in other ways, up to 1659 was of the order of 3,200; and for 1660-1689 of the order of 15,000, of which perhaps 450 died. So it would seem that more than 18,000 Friends suffered up to 1689. This is about the number of Friends in London Yearly Meeting today, and that with a population of 5-5½ million compared with 10 times that number today.

David Butler made an interesting analysis of Friends' sufferings 1650-1688. He analysed entries in Besse and, as there were many kinds of suffering, confined his analysis to two factors, imprisonment and fines, though without quantifying either. He produced time/quantity charts (not given here) which indicate that Oxfordshire, Warwickshire and Worcestershire had, perhaps, rather less than the national average with the emphasis on imprisonments rather than on fines. Gloucestershire was near the national average with the incidence of fines and imprisonments nearly equal; but Gloucestershire Friends were hard hit in the period 1670-85. Whatever the incidence throughout these four countries, it may not be quite the same in the corners of those four counties which make up our area; but it seems likely that our incidence was below average. The towns of Banbury and Evesham may have had patterns not very different from those of small towns elsewhere, though Evesham was hard hit before 1661. Of our rural meetings, it would seem that Campden and, particularly, Ettington fared worse than the others.

Organisation of Meetings and the building of Meeting Houses

George Fox set up MMs and QMs in about 1668. Few problems seem to have arisen here except in Worcestershire which appears to have got off to a rather shaky start. Redditch MM is, to us, a rather shadowy body which, after a few years, was absorbed into Evesham MM; and Armscote, Broadway, Netherton and Pershore seem to have had an uncertain status in that they either appeared at QM without being part of any MM or were one-meeting MMs. However, such anomalies were sorted out early in the 18th century.

The organisation has stood the test of time but it did involve a lot of travel for Friends and one must admire the many men and women who played their part. Even a local meeting might be four or more miles from home and it must be remembered that, for over 200 years, meetings were usually held twice on Sundays and once during the week. Further, many Friends were given tasks to do for their meeting (such as making some enquiry or collecting money) which could involve visiting many houses in a dispersed area. MM might be 15 or more miles away (e.g. Bicester to Banbury); QM could be 40 miles away (e.g. Campden to Frenchay near Bristol); the Bristol Yearly Meeting (see Chapter 6) perhaps 60 miles away; London YM up to 100 or more miles away; and a Circular Meeting (see Chapter 6) could be 150 miles away in Cornwall involving several days journey.

Until the coming of the railways the ways were dirty and dangerous; travel also took much time and some Friends could not afford to be many

THE TESTING YEARS

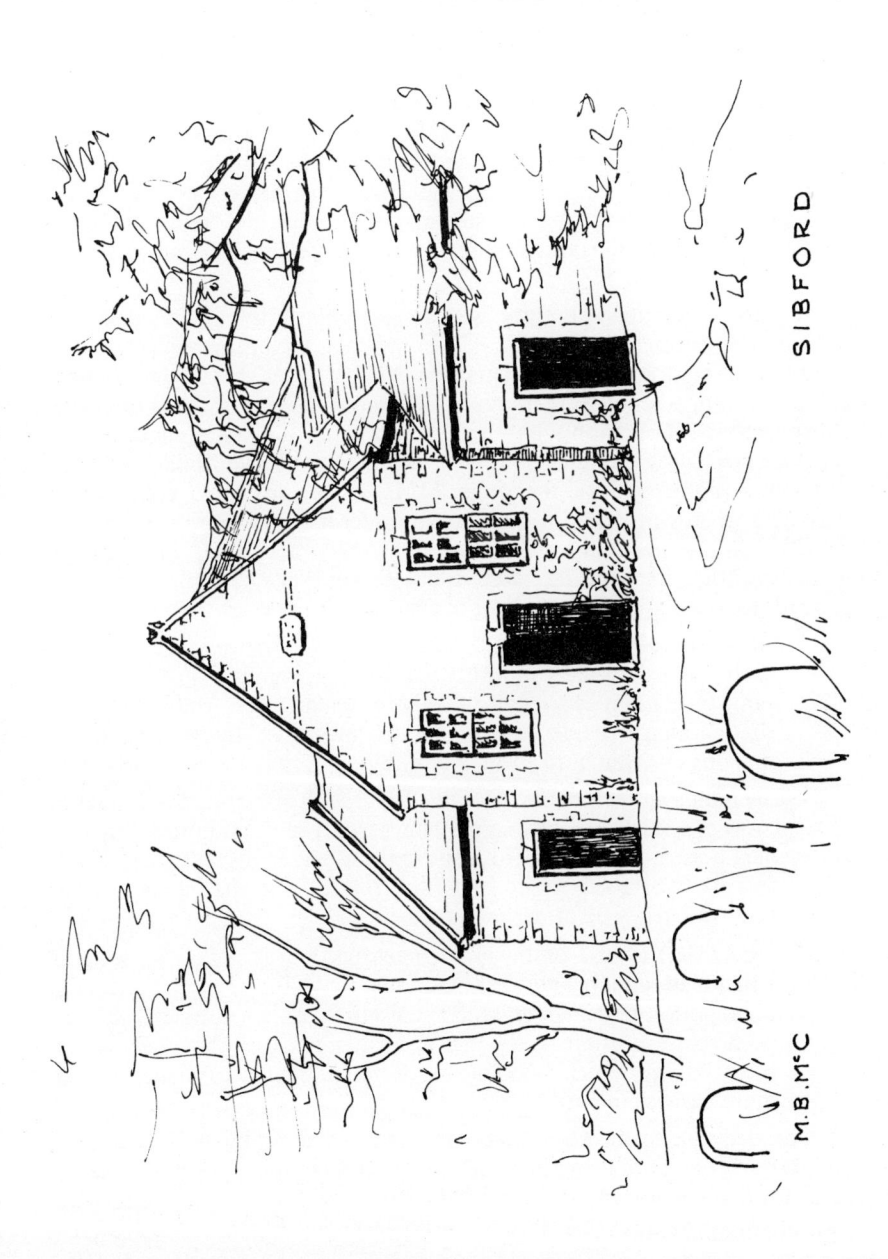

SIBFORD

M.B.McC

days away from the place where they earned their living. Horses were often used and some of our meeting houses had stables, but these were for the better-off and many walked. The local minutes in our area sometimes (but not often) record that a MM or QM was poorly attended, or even abandoned, because of bad weather; and there are some references to women's MMs or QMs not being held in some winter months. QMs complained that some distant meetings did not send representatives regularly; clearly high standards of service and personal discomfort were expected.

In the 1670s much thought was given to the role of women in the Society. In meetings for worship men and women sat together, with men in one block of seats and women in another ('The women's side'). On review, existing arrangements were judged satisfactory except for meetings for church affairs. It was thought best that women and men should have separate meetings, though working in harmony and meeting at the same time; this applied to local meetings, MMs, QMs and (later) YM. Over a period, women's functions became clear; they had a place in welfare and family matters generally, including marriage, and they had special responsibilities for dealing with sickness, old age, poverty and the education of the young. A minute of Oxfordshire QM in 1674 said:

> 'It is ordered by Friends . . . that the women in every division [i.e. each MM] shall meet monthly and make a women's meeting at the same time and place, when and where men do meet. And it is desired that all men Friends do persuade to, and assist, the women in the meetings as much as do in them lie'.

As the men's and women's meetings for church affairs met at the same time, it was possible to co-ordinate business and, in the minutes, one can almost hear notes being passed from one to the other. In his memoirs Joshua Lamb says about Sibford (in the 1870s and 1880s – but what he said would probably have been true of earlier times):

> 'Towards the end of business meetings it was usual for women Friends to send in a note asking if men Friends had any business for them; but it was an open secret that much of their time had already been spent in listening to what had taken place on the other side of the partition, which by no means excluded the voices of some of our more earnest members'.

The decision to have separate, but simultaneous, business meetings posed the difficulty of providing suitable accommodation. We know that in 1677 Campden Friends enlarged their meeting house and a loft with shutters was provided; this allowed for separate meetings for church affairs

THE TESTING YEARS

as well as providing for MM and QM when they came to visit. Adderbury built (at an unknown date) a small house close to the meeting house for such a purpose; and Shipston will probably have used their large upstairs space. No steps appear to have been taken to alter some meeting houses, for example Armscote and Ettington, and they probably used a room in a nearby house. The larger meeting houses at Banbury, Evesham and Sibford will have made some arrangements but, as all have been rebuilt, we do not know exactly what they were; though we know Banbury made some provision for women in 1681 and Sibford in 1736.

Not until 1689 were meeting houses acceptable under the law and until then their status was, to say the least, doubtful. However that did not stop Friends providing them. By the end of the 17th century the pattern of meetings and meeting houses in our area had largely been formed. Appendix 1 gives the detail but the broad picture is as follows:

	Date of first meeting	Date of meeting house (if any)
Adderbury	1656	1675
Alcester	1660	1677
Armscote	1655	1674-1705
Banbury	1654	1657 (moved structure to present site 1665)
Barton	1668	1668 or 1700
Bloxham	1665	None known
Bicester	1676	None known
Brailes	1657	1678-1686
Broadway	1662	None known
Campden	1656	1663 (bought – possibly same building as met in earlier)
Ettington	1660	1684
Evesham	1656	1676
Hook Norton	1668	1705
Long Compton	1661	1670
Milcombe	1665	None known
Netherton	1666	None known
North Newington	1666	None known
Kington	1690	1724(?)
Pershore	1662	Date unknown
Radway	1659	1702
Redditch	1660(?)	1708
Ridgeway	1677	None known

Cont.	Date of first meeting	Date of meeting house (if any)
Shipston	1655	1685
Shutford	1668	1689
Sibford	1668	1678-81
South Newington	1663	1692
Stow	1668	1719-1724

Broughton, Tadmarton and Lower Heyford had meetings before 1700 but there is no indication of dates; none had meeting houses as far as is known.

Links with Friends in America

Some Friends went from the Evesham area to New Jersey, USA, around 1680. There is no evidence of this in local minutes (many for the period have not survived) but we know something of this from New Jersey. In Burlington County, New Jersey, across the Delaware River from Philadelphia, there are various place names which obviously have their origin in our area, e.g. Evesham Township, Vale of Evesham, Camden (sic) and Mickleton (there are also other English place-names not from our area). Among those who emigrated were William Evens or Evans, and his wife Jean or Joan. We know from records here that they were married at Banbury Meeting in 1663 and somebody of his name had previously been active at South Newington Meeting. Around 1694, Evesham Meeting in New Jersey was being held in their house – the meeting is now known as Mount Laurel. William and Mary Evans visited Evesham (UK) in 1989; he is a ninth generation descendant of the William Evans referred to above, and she a descendant of John Woolman.

Quite apart from this link with New Jersey, we know that William Warner of Campden Meeting went to Philadelphia about the same time. Before emigrating he lived in Blockley and it is said that the name of the Blockley suburb of Philadelphia originated with him. Many Friends certainly emigrated from other meetings but there are no details.

Viscountess Conway

Viscountess Conway of Ragley Hall in Warwickshire was, perhaps, a surprising Quaker of her day. She was a daughter of Sir Heneage Finch and her eldest brother became Lord Chancellor and Earl of Nottingham. She married Edward, Viscount Conway of Ragley; he was rich and more interested in the life of a country squire than in her intellectual pursuits. She had a brilliant mind and was what would in a later age be called a 'bluestocking'. She was learned in Latin, Greek, theology and philosophy and much interested in the writings of Jacob Boehme of Silesia who was looked up to by many Quakers of her day. She corresponded with Isaac Penington, Robert Barclay, William Penn and George Fox. In 1677, Fox visited her at Ragley Hall (having come from Evesham on his way to Ridgeway) and found her 'tender and loving and willing to have me longer than I had freedom to stay'.

Dr. Henry More of Christ's College, Cambridge, an intellectual colleague, was alarmed at her interest in Friends but did not try to dissuade her. In a letter of 1675 she wrote to him: 'The reading of their [the Quakers'] books lately had, in a great measure, freed me from former prejudicate opinions; but their conversation doth much more reconcile me to them'. She had meetings in her chamber and changed her servants so that all were Quakers. A member of Alcester Meeting, she helped finance the Friends Meeting House at Aberdeen, through her link with Robert Barclay. She died in 1678.

Death of George Fox

George Fox died in 1691. Extracts from a long testimony by Oxfordshire QM give a reaction in our area.

'This is our testimony for that faithful and honourable servant of God, and minister of the everlasting Gospel of Jesus Christ, George Fox . . . [he] was a true and faithful labourer in the works and service the Lord called him into, in turning many from darkness into light, and from the power of Satan unto Christ – the power of the living God. And the Lord was with him and made his work to prosper in his hand insomuch that, in a short time, many that were as scattered sheep that had no shepherd were by him gathered . . . to Christ. Some of us can well remember when he first came up out of the north country into the southern parts; what a dread majesty and authority he was attended with, which made the hearts of many that beheld him to fear and tremble; for deceit and hypocricy could not stand before him. For many that were . . . sturdy oaks and tall cedars, high in notion and profession, were made to bow at the power of the word of his testimony. He had a piercing eye, and was wonderfully endowed with a spirit of discerning into the inward states and conditions of those he had to deal with.

As to his ministry, it was plain yet powerful, consisting much in prophetic openings declaring the day was come in which God was fulfilling the words and prophecies of his prophets. Not . . . with the words of man's natural wisdom but delivered in the Gospel simplicity, power and demonstration of God's eternal spirit . . . He was a man greatly beloved and much hated; for all good people that truly feared God, and loved Christ, the truth, that ever saw him or were acquainted with him – they loved him for the truth's sake and had an honourable esteem of him. Much . . . might we say of him as to his great sufferings and the blamelessness of his life and conversation . . . He was a blessing in the hands of the Lord to many thousands in this nation and other nations; whose memorial will live through generations to come and, through him, our sons have cause to bless the name of the Lord.'

CHAPTER 3

The Quiet Years (1700 to about 1860)

Quakers seen from the outside

It may be useful to look at an outside view – this is how the geneticist and historian Prof. C. D. Darlington, writing in the 1960s, summarised the Quaker phenomenon:

'It was during the Civil War that George Fox set out on his personal quest for truth by preaching the rejection of war. He transformed his followers into a society which then preserved itself. It did so both by its books of registration and by its intellectual and temperamental cohesion. All these things, together with their strict moral discipline, underlay the commercial and technical success of the Society of Friends. By the time they were known as Quakers, they were becoming a homogenous inbred group seeking to alleviate poverty but needing to turn outside their community if they were to find it.

How had the Quakers improved their position? Their repudiation of pretended beliefs and meaningless ceremonies, as well as their respect for women, inevitably led them to drop their least intelligent, and also least successful, adherents to whom ritual, formality and status meant most. The Quaker practice of logical severity was pre-adapted to commercial success and, by its example, led to a revolution in commercial methods which spread throughout all Protestant societies.'

Changes in Britain: 'Quiet Friends'

The 18th and early 19th centuries were, for most in Britain, a time of social, industrial and commercial change. The energies released by the William and Mary settlement brought a new vigour to the country and there was much emphasis on new ways, and many of the new ways brought prosperity. Within a generation from 1700, England had become a leading commercial nation and, within two, the initiator of the industrial revolution which, in time, changed the world. Many of the old features of society were swept away and many people became prosperous and some very rich; but there was also hardship, poverty and insecurity in both towns and country.

The Test Act and other measures debarred Friends (and other dissenters) from all public offices including the House of Commons; and they were likewise excluded from universities and most schools because they would not take the communion of the Anglican Church (these restrictions were removed progressively during the 19th century). As Friends were, by inclination, self-reliant and believed in hard work and honest dealings, those of them who might have gone to university or sought public office turned instead to industry, commerce and the professions.

The craftsman expanded his trade and might come to own a considerable business. Others started at the bottom of some business, often a Quaker family concern, and worked their way towards the top. Scientists such as John Dalton revealed natural laws which led to new technologies adopted by Quakers and others; families like the Darbys of Coalbrookdale became initiators of the industrial revolution; bankers (such as the Gilletts of Banbury) and insurance underwriters (the Friends Provident were pioneers) looked to the long term and became enablers of progress and business success. The Quaker practice of having fixed prices for goods for sale, instead of haggling to agree a price, was at first looked at askance by the public but, before long, was widely supported and followed.

The other side of the coin was the Quaker withdrawal from 'the world' in religious and private life. They were pacifists in a military-minded world; they would not pay tithes and this continued to alienate them from the clergy and some of the gentry; they rejected fashionable women's clothes for plain grey dresses, white scarves and poke bonnets (and broadcloth and wide-brimmed hats for men); and they would not use titles or flowery phrases but stuck to 'thee' and 'thou'. The arts were largely rejected because many of the books on art and song were deemed unsuitable and because there was the serious work of the Lord to be done; thus, practising a musical instrument, or drawing a picture, was to waste valuable time. It must be remembered that many Friends were heavily engaged in running their meetings and this burden absorbed energies which might have been used in other ways.

Thus, on the one hand, Friends stood aside from many activities of their day and tended to withdraw from society but, on the other hand, many were entrepreneurs and innovators whose energies brought prosperity to the country as well as themselves. One has only to study the writings and minutes of the period to realise that the two approaches were not in any serious competition. Though prosperous Quaker merchants were, inevitably, much 'in the world', they were also separated from it in much of their private lives; they kept to Quaker precepts, played a substantial part in the business life of their meetings and used their wealth and energies in furthering Quaker causes. Some may be inclined to discount Friends for their 'quiet' years; one can only say that they sought to change the world and, when this proved beyond their strength, adhered to their own principles in the face of much difficulty. In doing so, they showed what honesty of purpose could achieve and how it could be combined with a prosperous business, was indeed a necessary concomitant of prosperity.

Decline and new growth

In the 18th and early 19th centuries the numbers of Quakers declined, a substantial cause being that disownments exceeded convincements (new members). Disownments are considered below but it would seem that our meetings were not particularly keen on accepting new members until well into the 19th century. Applications were considered at length, perhaps over several meetings, and (judging by the minutes) some applications got 'lost' and were never finally dealt with. And even acceptances could sound a little grudging. Banbury MM 1702: 'Thomas Wagstaff having drawings to come to the meeting and offer himself to serve truth; Friends having nothing against him but that he may serve truth as a member of this meeting'.

The other main reason for decline in our area was rural depopulation. The repeal of the Corn Laws allowed imports of cheap cereals and there were other political and economic factors at work – for example, the silk industry at Blockley and Campden was destroyed by changes in import permits. Most of our Quakers were in work related to agriculture (see Appendix 2) and many had to move away because of lack of work. Some went to the towns but others emigrated. It has been estimated that in 1700 there were 20,000 Quakers in Pennsylvania alone and, thus, many more in North America as a whole. We have no figures for our area but the subject of emigration crops up in the records – for example, a reference to emigration to America from Brailes in the mid-18th century and to Australia from Banbury in the mid-19th century.

The decline was most noticeable in the rural area of Warwickshire South MM. Shipston MM and Campden and Stow MM, which originated in the early days, were never strong and in 1790 they merged with the previously small Warwickshire South MM; the enlarged body had 10 meetings (excluding Armscote) but, by 1890, there were only 2 meetings – Ettington and Shipston. For much of the 18th and 19th centuries they were telling QM that their resources were inadequate and that they had difficulty in meeting the needs of their sick and poor; that the cost of maintaining meeting houses was more than they could manage; and that the select committee of elders and ministers (in 1856) had only two members who felt themselves 'unable from advanced age and declining health' to continue. In 1885 it was reported that meetings had

> 'with little exception been regularly held and we can thankfully acknowledge that in meeting together we have felt both strengthened and comforted. We cannot report any organised religious work directly under the care of this meeting but some of our members take part in such charitable work as may be around them'.

But this low ebb of their existence was replaced by the flood tide of adult school and other work a few years later – see Chapter 5. Decline was not confined to Warwickshire South MM. Evesham MM had (probably) eight meetings in 1725, four in 1800 and only one in 1811. Banbury MM had nine to fourteen meetings in 1700 (some dates are uncertain), six in 1800 and five in 1900 – the Banbury area was the most prosperous part of the MM.

In our area, iron ore was worked near Banbury but there were no iron works or substantial factories and, apart from agricultural work and attendant trades, little commercial work. An extensive canal system built up, and a railway system later, but there is no evidence that Friends were involved in running them. A profession which left its mark was clock and watch making, a cottage industry run by a small number of skilled men which flourished until the middle of the 19th century, when it was affected by shelf-clocks imported from America. Thomas Gilkes of Sibford Gower was a pioneer clockmaker towards the end of the 17th century. Richard Gilkes started a business at Adderbury about 1735 and made clocks of an old-fashioned design which hung on the wall and, later long-case ('grandfather') clocks. John Fardon set up business in Deddington which was later taken over by Thomas Harris of Sibford Ferris who moved the work to Bloxham. Later, it was run by John Fardon II and Thomas Fardon (a blacksmith) who, among other things, made the clock for Deddington church. John Gilkes was a clockmaker at Shipston in the mid-18th century and, in the next century, Richard Gilkes made clocks with painted dials at Sibford Gower. There were those of the name of Gilkes at Chipping Campden who probably made clocks, and also Bevingtons who certainly did – this family may also have been tanners as they had hides taken from them by distraint.

The Gillett family were, from at least the early 18th century, sheep farmers of Upper Brailes and there is still a 'Gilletts Lane' there. They prospered and went in for wool-combing and then, about the beginning of the 19th century, engaged in the plush business – which was the only cottage industry of consequence in the neighbourhood. ('Plush' was the name for various types of velvet cloth made from cotton, wool and silk and used for rich clothing.) Joseph Ashby Gillett was the son of William Gillett who had started the plush business and, in 1824, he went into banking – initially at Shipston and then in Banbury where he bought the Banbury New Bank. He bought property in and around Banbury and was engaged in activities such as agricultural machinery. Under his care the plush industry of Brailes flourished and, in 1838, he had about 150 looms there with 20 girls working whole-time with perhaps 100 outworkers. He also built a plush factory at Banbury (and there was also a factory at Shutford). The trade later went into decline. J. A. Gillett died in 1853 and his sons Alfred and Charles took over the business. Before and after that date branches of the bank were set up at Brackley, Chipping Norton, Woodstock, Witney and Oxford. In 1867 Alfred and Charles went into the London discount market as Gillett Bros. & Co. As with most commercial enterprises there were good years and bad but as a family they flourished. In 1919 their banking interests were merged with Barclays Bank.

The Gillett family were active in Banbury and other local meetings. They were involved with various philanthropic activities and helped set up clothing clubs (through which people could save up to buy clothes) and soup-kitchens in hard times. They were concerned with Quaker and other schools, including Sibford Friends School opened in 1842. Joseph Ashby Gillett in particular was recognised as an independent man and was asked to serve in various capacities. For example when, in 1845, there were many schemes in the air for the bringing of a railway to Banbury, Joseph was asked to chair a meeting to resolve the issue. Banbury was clearly a Quaker centre of some significance for much of the 19th century in particular. In 1829 Joseph John Gurney (brother of Elizabeth Fry) wrote 'In the country Friends are reduced and scattered. Here [in Banbury] they are an increasing, and very comfortable Society, and it has been a pleasure to become acquainted with them'.

As will be seen from Chapter 5, many of our Friends were, by the end of the 19th century, working on adult school and mission work; this was true of Banbury but there was also work on temperance, in particular, from the mid-century. Samuel Beezley was a Quaker businessman (he started the manufacture of 'Banbury Cakes') and evangelist who founded the temperance movement in the town; James Cadbury also worked for temperance and Charles Gillett was a leader of the anti-vaccination league. William Biggs, a chemist, was involved in furthering the work of the Mechanics' Institute. John Head, a Quaker hosier, fitted up a 'large commodious room' in Parson's St. in 1842 which served the temperance movement for half a century.

Sufferings after the Toleration Act 1689

After 1689, punitive action against Quakers was virtually confined to distraint of goods for non-payment of tithes or church rates, or for not joining the militia. The militia laws were complicated but, broadly speaking, when it was desired to increase the numbers in the militia, action could be taken in two ways. If the local parish agreed, a rate was charged on all householders and there was a call for volunteers; those who volunteered could get a payment from the rates. If any Friend refused to pay such a rate, his goods were distrained to cover the amount due and cost of collection. If the parish did not agree to call for volunteers, or if not enough came forward, a special register of eligible men was drawn up and people chosen by ballot. A Friend so selected could appoint and pay a substitute to go in his place (for this he would be in trouble as such action was much frowned on by YM) or he could refuse to take any action. In the latter instance, the magistrates could appoint a substitute and charge the Friend the cost of doing this and, if he did not pay, then there was distraint of his goods.

The figures given below aim to highlight two aspects of the incidence of distraints – the varying pattern in a locality and the changing pattern in the 19th century.

Meetings (in our area) in Worcestershire QM 1723-28:

Meeting	Number of incidents	Total value (£) of distraints	Value (£) per incidents	Average no. of incidents per annum
Alcester	3	5	1.66	0.12
Broadway*	103	284	2.75	4.12
Evesham	1	4	4.00	0.04
Kington*	11	21	1.90	0.44
Netherton*	10	10	1.00	0.40
Norton Beauchamp*	0	0	0	0
Pershore	86	74	0.86	3.44
Redditch	0	0	0	0
Ridgeway*	0	0	0	0
Shipston	168	586	3.49	6.72

*= small villages.

Almost all the distraints were for agricultural produce and it may be thought not surprising that a small town like Evesham had a low incidence. However, the largest town, Worcester (not shown as it is outside our area), had the most incidents. So it seems that the number of incidents and the size of the distraints varied a great deal and there was no clear pattern. This presumably was due to haphazard approaches by the collectors or to haphazard return of incidents to be recorded, or both.

Figures of distraints for Banbury MM, for the 48 years to 1812, are given below but it should first be explained that, in some times and places, a cash sum (for perhaps a tenth of the value of the goods distrained) was later returned by the sequestrator to the Friend involved. The number of these 'rebates' in Banbury MM increased with the years; it may be that the aim was to try to defend the sequestrator from any charge that he had seized goods to a greater value than was justified.

Sufferings by distraint of goods, Banbury MM 1794-1841

Number of All Distraints		12 years 1794-1805	12 years 1806-1817	12 years 1818-1829	12 years 1830-1841	48 years 1794-1841
Farm – livestock grain etc.		39	15	30	48	132
Household – furniture etc.		6	10	23	84	123
Craft – leather etc.		0	6	9	14	29
Totals		45	31	62	146	284
Value of Tithe Distraints	£(total)	117	140	234	431	922
(Cash returned)	£(total)	(8)	(10)	(133)	(41)	(192)
Value of Militia Distraints	£(total)	151	42	42	0	235
(Cash returned)	£(total)	(11)	(10)	(5)	0	(26)
Net Value of Distraints (Tithe & Militia)		249	162	138	390	939

ETTINGTON

M.B.McC

In a number of cases, the net value of what was taken was more (sometimes much more) than the amount due and only in a small number of cases does the value seem to have been less than required. The value placed on some goods (e.g. a table or a pair of used shoes) must often have been little more than a guess; the owner and sequestrator would have difficulty in agreeing what was right. The number of distraints fluctuated considerably, but it will be seen that the value of tithe distraints increased sharply in the latter periods; and that the number of distraints of household goods was initially small but increased greatly over the years.

An unusual case of sufferings by distraint in lieu of tithes was recorded in the minutes of Shipston MM:

'An account of the sufferings of Alice Wyatt brought in here of contents as follows. "Taken from Alice Wyatt of Tredingham in the county of Gloucester in the year 1763. Wheat, barley, pulses and vetches to the value of £3.18.0. Taken by John Wyatt for the use of John Taylor, priest of Tredingham aforesaid, as being his pretended due; all taken without my consent. As witness my hand, Alice Wyatt." (The place may have been Tredington, then in Worcestershire.)'

This is unusual in two ways. First, the MM was not then recording the details of any sufferings in their minutes – but they made an exception for Alice. Secondly, they made the same minute (with virtually only the date changed) in every year from at least 1758 (when the minute book started) for 12 years. It is clear that Alice felt very strongly about the seizure of her goods (exactly the same crops, to the same value, each year) and much wanted the MM to record it.

In the 1830s tithes in kind were, by law, commuted into rents payable to the tithe owner (ecclesiastical or lay impropriator as the case might be). This was of little help to Friends as they still refused to make tithe payments, and goods were distrained in lieu. In 1868 church rates were abolished. In 1873 YM decided to leave it to individuals to decide what they did about tithes – though the Society maintained its stand against ecclesiastical usurpation. Few Friends seem to have struggled against tithes for long, so that 200 years of sufferings by distraint were virtually at an end. As to tithes themselves, they were in effect abolished in the 20th century.

'Is he of good conversation?'

For many years the question – 'Is he (or she) of good conversation, is a moral life being followed?' was asked when arrangements were being made to transfer a Friend to another meeting because of a house-move; when it was necessary to establish whether parties to a proposed marriage were 'clear'; and when considering whether somebody should be disowned. Such matters took up a lot of time at MMs until the second half of the 19th century.

Membership

Membership has always had its obligations. A Friend is expected to play his or her part in the running of the meeting and support it financially but there were, at one time, potential social benefits in that the meeting looked after those of their members who were sick or poor – and, in the 18th century most of our meetings had poor. This was an attitude stemming from the Poor Laws, the essence of which was that a parish looked after 'its own' who were in need, but did not take responsibility for those belonging to another parish. This applied to all visitors but, once an incomer had paid taxes in the locality or done work for the parish (perhaps had been a constable), he or she was then accepted – 'settled' was the word used – and became a resident like any other. Friends followed such principles, and retained them until 1861, and Quakers who fell on evil times were only eligible for benefit from their own MM. If they were, for example, taken ill while outside the compass of their MM, the MM in which they were temporarily residing would doubtless help but was free to claim the cost from the visitor's own MM. The rules were complicated but the essence was clear: an MM was only responsible for those 'settled' with them.

When a man (the same procedure applied to a woman) went to live outside the compass of his MM, he was expected to ask for his membership to be transferred. Today, this is done by a simple form but, for many years, it was an important matter to be looked at carefully. The MM from which he had come would make enquiries on his way of life, whether he was free of debt and whether he had any marriage entanglements. A report would be made and, if all was well, a certificate (in effect a letter) would be drawn up saying (usually 'as far as is known') that he was free of debt, etc. This might be quite a long statement and be signed by, perhaps, 20 Friends; it may have been thought right for many to sign it to indicate that all were satisfied on the facts. The receiving MM would make its own enquiries and, unless anything untoward emerged, accept the transfer. If, however, either MM found anything against the man, a long correspondence between the two might follow.

A typical, but short, transfer certificate from 1776 read:

'From our Monthly Meeting held at Adderbury for Banbury Division in the County of Oxford [i.e. from Banbury MM]. To the

Monthly Meeting of Friends to be held at Campden or elsewhere in that Division of the County of Gloucester [i.e. Campden and Stow MM]. Dear Friends, whereas Elizabeth Franklin a member hereof, but is now removed into the compass of yours, a certificate has been requested of this meeting on her behalf. Therefore, this may certify, after due enquiry being made, it appears she was of a sober life and conversation, and free from marriage entanglements. As such we recommend her to your tender regard desiring the growth in the truth. With the salutations of love we remain your Friends and brethren. Signed in and on behalf of our said meeting by' . . . six women and seventeen men with their names recorded in full in the minutes.

In 1820-21 Joseph Gibbs, thought to be a member of Leighton ('Hogstyend') MM, was taken ill while in Banbury and given help at a cost of about £35; Leighton MM were asked to pay for it 'he not having a settlement' in Banbury. Leighton did not accept that he belonged to their MM; letters passed and visits were made but agreement was not reached. Leighton appealed to their QM who supported them. Banbury MM, with the support of their QM, appealed to YM. But at this point commonsense prevailed and the two MMs agreed on the proportion each should pay.

Marriages

Marriages, by comparison, raised few difficulties. The couple who wanted to marry went to the MM wherein they wished the marriage to take place. Both would appear in person and, if one did not live in that MM, he or she would produce a letter from his or her MM. Both MMs wanted to know if the parents approved and if the parties were of good conversation. On getting affirmative reports, usually at the next meeting, permission was given for the marriage to take place at a meeting house and two Friends would be appointed to see that good order was preserved. Though a marriage was doubtless recognised as a happy occasion, it was essential that a MM be sure that all was 'clear' and so tensions could arise. Joshua Lamb of Sibford in his memoirs said 'One of the most trying regulations of those days [mid-late 19th century] was that the notice of an intended marriage had to be given by the prospective bridegroom himself [to the MM] and, in one instance at any rate, a well-known couple married at the Registry Office rather than face the ordeal'.

One example (from the minutes of Warwickshire South MM) describes what usually happened.

1778. 'Joseph Gibbins a member of the North Monthly Meeting in this county, son of Thomas Gibbins of (Tregar ?) in Monmouthshire, and Martha Bevington, daughter of Martha Bevington of Ettington, laid their intention of marriage before this meeting. Joseph Gibbins produced a certificate of his father's consent and Martha Bevington, being present, signified her daughter's proceedings are with her consent. We therefore refer said proposals to the consideration of our next.'

Next month. 'Joseph Gibbins and Martha Bevington were present at this meeting and express the continuation of their taking each other in marriage. The said Joseph Gibbins producing a certificate from the Monthly Meeting of which he is a member to inform, under enquiry, he is clear from other engagements of like kind – and therefore, as nothing appears to obstruct their proceeding, we leave them at liberty to accomplish their said intentions according to the good order used amongst us. And we appoint William Marshall and Jeffrey Bevington to attend on the day of marriage to see that good order is preserved and to make report thereon to our next.'

Following month. 'William Marshall and Jeffrey Bevington attended the marriage [at Ettington] of Joseph Gibbins and Martha Bevington – one of whom informs this meeting it was conducted in a becoming orderly manner.'

Joseph and Martha Gibbins were the great grandparents of Wilfrid Gibbins who was, in 1990, Clerk of Broad Campden Meeting. Joseph (he was then a 'button maker') was 22 when they were married, Martha 19. They had 16 children who survived childbirth and they died in 1811 and 1827 respectively. Joseph was Clerk of YM in 1797 and 1802, and a founder of the Midland Bank.

Disownments

Disownments were a feature of Friends' dealings until the 1860s/70s. Though they caused much difficulty and heartache, the step was never taken lightly and the incidence should not be exaggerated. Some figures are:

Cause of Disownment	Evesham MM 1699-1812 (113 years)	Banbury MM 1785-1789 (5 years)	1833-1837 (5 years)
Immorality	4	0	0
Drunkenness	3	8	0
Bankruptcy	4	4	2
Marrying-out	21	14	2
Other reasons	3	10	0
	35	36	4
	Roughly one every 3 years	Roughly 7 a year	Less than one a year

The number of disownments in the 18th century was very much higher in Banbury than in Evesham but it was a much larger MM; and disownments in Banbury were much lower in the 1830s.

Some examples of various kinds of disownment:

In 1680 Thomas Bailes (or Bayliss) of Adderbury was criticised by the Oxfordshire QM who regretted that he kept his hat on when 'Friends in the meeting are supplicating the Lord in public prayer' and that he also told 'people of the world' of weaknesses he found among Friends. (At that time keeping one's hat on while another prayed aloud in meeting signified lack of unity with the speaker.) At a later QM he sought to justify himself but it was considered that he 'continued in obstinacy and wilfulness' and he was eventually disowned.

Warwickshire South MM 1766. 'Whereas William Gibbs of Stowerton hath gone to the priest for a wife, contrary to our established rules, we therefore have no longer unity with him, or acknowledge him as a member of our Society; until by demonstration and unaffected repentance for his said outgoings, he regains fellowship.'

Warwickshire South MM 1758. 'Whereas the conduct of Thomas Soden and his wife, late of Brailes, has been a great blemish to the truth they having made profession in their conveying goods away which belonged to their creditors without their knowledge – and also removing themselves and their children contrary to repeated advice. Therefore we, the people called Quakers, have no longer unity with the said Thomas Soden and his wife until they, by amendment of life, do their evident demonstrations of sorrow for all their outgoings – which we earnestly desire.'

In 1805 Sarah Hemmings of Banbury was visited by MM representatives about her non-attendance at meetings. It was said that she 'did not in the least condemn her inconsistent conduct' and she wrote saying that she wished to withdraw from membership. However, she was not allowed to resign but was disowned.

Warwickshire South MM in 1808 recorded that 'This meeting is informed that William Cork and his wife, of Campden, have by their conduct brought a great reproach on both themselves and our Religious Society by having two children born at a very early period after their marriage'. After a visit to them 'They appeared sensible of their misconduct but, as the case is of so reproachable a nature, believing it our indisputable duty for the clearance of truth to testify against them'. They were disowned but must have continued going to meetings for worship as they were accepted back into membership a few years later.

George and Hannah Gillett of Warwickshire South MM went to Australia and a certificate was issued 'They are hereby recommended to the Christian sympathy of those amongst whom they may come'. In 1863 MM had their certificate returned by an Australian Meeting which had visited them. 'The interview was a lengthened one but was not considered satisfactory. [They] seem to value their membership chiefly in consequence of their early associations and not from any belief in the doctrines and principles of our Religious Society; nor did they hold out any hope to us that they would in future attend our meetings for worship, although we pointed out to them the necessity for doing so if they had a desire to retain their membership.' They were disowned by Warwickshire South MM and when, four years later, they asked for their children to remain on the MM list, this was refused.

(See also item 18 of Appendix 1 – a disownment for bad behaviour.)

It must not be thought that action was always punitive. For example:

Shipston MM in 1755. 'John Jephcut and Hannah Tapling, servants to Joshua Ashley and members of this meeting, not having the fear of the Lord before their eyes, have had carnal knowledge of each other whereby an illegal child is born. And this meeting, having taken the affair into consideration, do appoint [two Friends] to endeavour to bring them to a sense of their crime and to acquaint them that, unless they give evidence of sincere repenting, and acknowledge and condemn their fault in writing in a public manner to this meeting – so that the acknowledgement may be as public as the scandal they have brought on our Society – they will be publicly disowned.' At the next meeting it was reported that they acknowledged their crime and seemed penitent and 'having since taken each other in marriage . . . this meeting suspends further consideration against them'. They were, presumably, married by a priest but the meeting seems to have chosen to overlook this.

Warwickshire South MM 1822. 'After considering the case of John Bissel's failure to pay his just debts, and fulfill his engagements punctually, this meeting is of the opinion that it is necessary to bear a decided testimony against such conduct; but, as some circumstances lead us to think favourably of his intentions, we are inclined to act with as much charity and forebearance as we can do consistently with the discharge of our duty' and his case was suspended until the meeting were satisfied with his conduct.

There were potentially serious problems which did not lead to disownment.

A long-running 'breach of love' was recorded at Adderbury by Banbury MM in 1822-26. It was between Richard and Esther Lamb who was the widow of Richard's brother; they were together engaged in some trade. The dispute was (partly at least) about property and, after a time, MM arranged for arbitration by representatives of YM. The arbitrators, and also some later arbitration, found for Esther; but then there was a dispute about implementation. In 1862 the dispute was still rumbling on and the ownership of a house seems to have been settled in Esther's favour. Then Esther's son, William, seems to have joined the feud and broke into Richard's property in an endeavour to recover some amount outstanding. Richard eventually paid up; and William apologised and made some recompense. And nobody was disowned – but it must have been a possibility in the mind of the MM.

By the first half of the 19th century, the Society was clearly in decline as far as numbers were concerned (some feared it would be a terminal decline) because of disownments and some unduly restrictive rules. After much heart-searching, many of the rules and practices, which had guided Friends for years, were discarded or greatly modified. The largest number of disownments was for marrying-out and this mainly arose from a Friend wanting to marry a non-Friend; as, legally, this could not be done in a meeting house, they went to a priest to be married. From 1860, non-Friends could legally be married in a meeting house and, as a result, disownment for marrying-out declined rapidly. Action was taken to ensure that the incidence of other disownments was greatly reduced. Before long, disownment virtually ceased.

Endpiece

Perhaps we might end this chapter, as we began it, with an outside view of Friends. This one is by Christopher Smart in 'Rejoice in the Lamb' published in the 18th century.

> 'For it is not good to wear anything on the head,
> For a man should put no obstacle,
> Between his head and the blessing of Almighty God.
> Lord have mercy on the Quakers.'

CHAPTER 4

Changing Times

The number of Quakers and attendance at Meetings

William C. Braithwaite thought that in England and Wales there were between 30 and 40,000 Quakers in 1659 and about 40-50,000 in the 1670s; but he notes that others have suggested much larger numbers. It seems that numbers continued to increase despite much persecution.

Michael Watts estimated that there were about 40,000 Quakers in England around 1718, or 0.73% of the then population of 5.4 million, with 672 meetings. (By comparison, he puts the number of Presbyterians at about 180,000 or 3.3% of the population.) He estimates the number of Quakers in the whole of the four counties in which our area lies, and the number of meetings, to be as set out below; but it must be emphasised that he is dealing with an area much bigger than ours.

	Estimated number of Quakers		Estimated number of meetings
Gloucestershire	960	(0.7% of county population)	22
Oxfordshire	780	(0.9% ,,)	14
Warwickshire	690	(0.7% ,,)	20
Worcestershire	730	(0.7% ,,)	15

It has been suggested that in 1800 there were less than 20,000 Quakers but nobody is at all sure. We come to firmer ground in 1862 when the first annual count of Friends (the 'tabular statement') was introduced. The figure was about 13,600 adults. One might conclude that the orders of magnitude were:

Date	Number of Quakers
1660	30-40,000
1675	40-50,000
1700	40,000 or more

Cont.

Date	Number of Quakers	
1800	20,000	
1860	13,600	3,000 attenders
1900	17,300	7,800 attenders) Some, but not all,
1910	19,500	7,500 attenders) at mission meetings
1918	20,000	7,000 attenders) probably included.
1989	18,000	8,700 adult attenders and 5,200 children.

Until fairly late in the 19th century, the larger of our meetings worshipped twice on Sundays and once on a weekday. Smaller meetings tended progressively to drop, first, the weekday meetings and, then, those on Sunday evenings; in large and some small meetings, the Sunday evening gathering often changed from a meeting for worship to a mission meeting. By the end of the 1914-18 war, the pattern (apart from a few mission meetings tending to decline) was meetings for worship on Sunday mornings only; but Banbury and Shipston had rather more than this for a time.

In 1814 the Government arranged for a census to be taken of those worshipping (in all denominations) on a particular Sunday; the exercise was repeated by YM (for Quaker Meetings only) in 1904, 1909 and 1914. The figures for meetings in our area are given below but it must be emphasised that these were *attendances* on that Sunday (or in some few cases an average of estimated attendances over the last 12 months) and included both members and attenders. Figures did not include children in the earlier years but probably did in the latter. Those at adult schools should not have been included. It will be appreciated that these figures are not the same as for members 'on the books'.

	1841 Mng Aft	1904 Mng Aft Miss	1909 Mng Aft Miss	1914 Mng Aft Miss
Adderbury	16 —	— — —	4 — —	Closed
Armscote	Closed	Closed	Closed	1 — —
Badsey	Not open	30 — 61	42 — 105	48 — 57
Banbury (Horsefair)	60 39	43 26 —	29 12 —	33 9 —
Banbury (Neithrop Mission)	Not open	11 — 67	22 — 56	9 — 29
Campden	4 —	Closed	Closed	Closed
Ettington	8 7	4 — —	3 — —	6 — —

Cont.	1841		1904			1909			1914		
	Mng	Aft	Mng	Aft	Miss	Mng	Aft	Miss	Mng	Aft	Miss
Evesham	21	14	31	—	59	23	—	55	23	—	40
Hook Norton	11	—	—	—	—	—	—	—	5	—	—
Littleton	Not open		38	—	96	18	—	82	17	—	70
Sibford*	112	—	91	53	—	116	100	—	134	108	—
Shipston	24	—	9	—	42	11	—	60	9	—	43
S.Newington	—	—	—	9	—	—	2	—	Closed		

Notes: Mng = morning meeting
Aft = afternoon or evening meeting
Miss = mission meeting
*Sibford's figures swollen by those from Sibford School.
Hook Norton and S. Newington were not meeting every Sunday.

The history of Armscote and its General Meeting (1655 to 1991)

The history of Armscote is an unusual one and it seems right to bring it all together in one place. Its early origins are obscure but it may be that its General Meeting, which has been in existence for perhaps 200 years, arose out of one of the Circular Meetings (see Chapter 6) in the 17th century.

The first report of a meeting there was in 1655 but there is little information until 1673 when George Fox visited it. He was recently back from America, and in poor health, and was on the way to Swarthmoor Hall; his wife Margaret, her daughter Rachel and Margaret's son-in-law Thomas Lower (who had married Mary Fell) were with him. They had been with William Penn at Rickmansworth and they then stayed with Bray D'Oyly at Adderbury. Fox said 'And there I set up in the country two or three more meetings, Friends being very plentiful in those counties and truth very much increasing'. Then they went to John Halford's house at Armscote 'where we had a very large and precious meeting in his barn and the Lord's powerful presence was amongst us'; this was the barn of the Manor House where John Halford lived and almost certainly not the present meeting house.

After the meeting, Fox and his Friends went to the Manor where, in the parlour, Justice Parker (Recorder of Evesham) came to them with a priest. Fox and Lower were arrested for having a meeting 'to the number of 200 or thereabouts' and sent to Worcester gaol. There is a local tradition that Fox hid from the justice in a 'priest hole'. This can be firmly denied both because Quakers worshipped openly and did not hide from the authorities, and because Fox specifically says he was 'Sitting in the parlour discussing with some Friends when the justice arrived'. That part of the country was

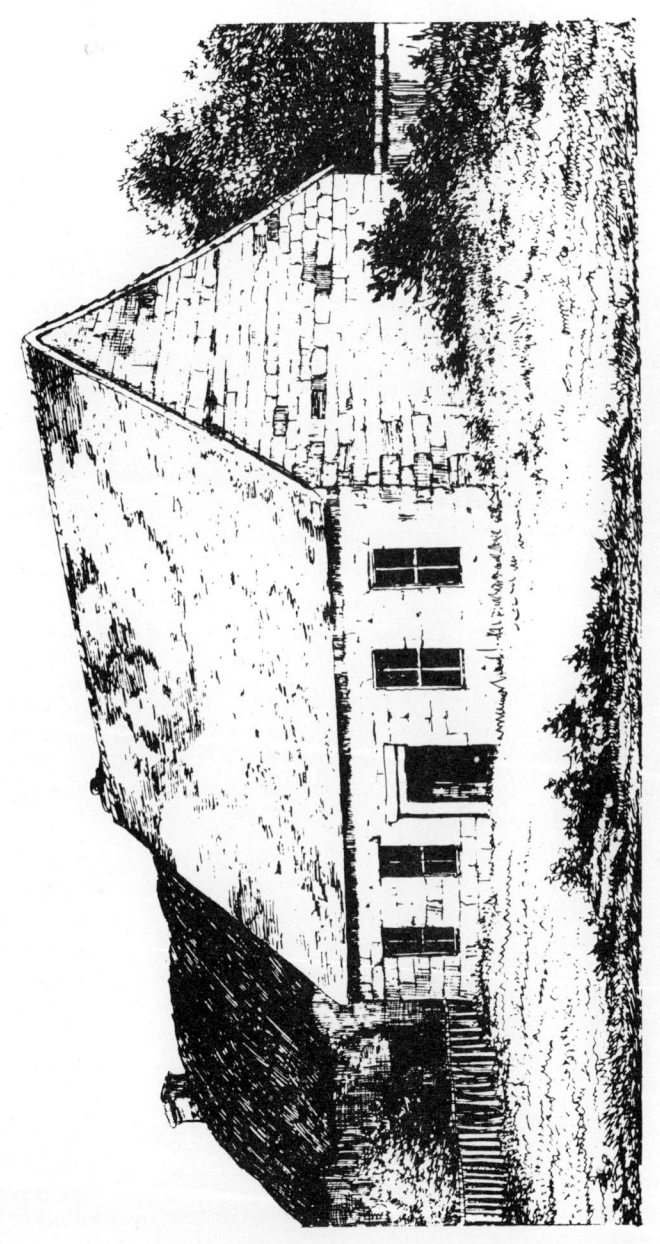

ARMSCOTE — FROM A STEEL ENGRAVING (PROBABLY ABOUT 1800)

connected with the Gunpowder Plot – could it be that local tradition has confused him with another 'G.F.' who may have been at Armscote, and in difficulty, some years earlier – one Guy Fawkes?

In 1674 Friends bought the present site and it is probable that there was a barn already there which was used for meetings, and that this was then improved to form an adequate meeting house. In any case, the present meeting house was available by 1705 with a burial ground. It remains today much as it must have been then (though a verandah was added later) with a stand opposite the door and no loft. It is not known how often meetings for worship were held there, or whether the term 'General Meeting' was then in use, but it must have been a flourishing meeting as representatives were sent to Worcestershire QM where they appeared in their own right – i.e. they were not listed as part of some MM. But it does not seem to have prospered long as, in 1714, it dropped out of the QM records and became part of Shipston; by 1721 it was reported that there were only four meetings a year at Armscote and, by 1800, there were only two a year. These were on the first Sundays in May and August – the latter being called the 'Armscote General Meeting'. By 1806 there was only the General Meeting in August of each year.

In 1863 Warwickshire South MM discussed with Warwick, Leicester and Stafford QM the future of Armscote and the QM sent representatives to visit it. They said:

'On reaching the meeting house half an hour before the time of the meeting . . . we found a number of persons gathered round the premises, others continued to arrive, some of them having walked a considerable distance. The interest shown on the occasion brought its importance closely to our minds.

Many Friends arriving from various parts of the surrounding country, and neighbouring QMs, and some from a considerable distance. The house was quite filled, the company was mostly of the labouring class or small farmers [and] included both old and young persons. Their conduct was becoming, and in many cases exemplary, about 100 being unable to gain admittance and most remained outside near the doors and windows. After the conclusion of the meeting, as well as before it commenced, tracts were freely distributed and eagerly received'.

About 40 Friends met afterwards. 'All seemed agreed that the meeting held the more season of divine favour being well attended. They also concurred in the feeling that it would be a serious matter lightly to close so open a door to those who may be willing to seek after truth and labour in it. A little enquiry was made of persons living at Armscote, respecting the behaviour of people during the rest of the day, but we were informed by them that most of the attenders of the meeting returned directly home and that there was no misconduct such as had been feared by some Friends'.

The QM said that the report 'excited much interest' and agreed that Armscote General Meeting should continue and be under QM auspices. Warwick, Leicester and Stafford QM, and later Berks and Oxon QM and Western QM, appointed representatives to attend each year.

A further report to QM in 1875 said:

'A good meeting was held and was largely attended, the house being quite full and many standing outside; some concern was felt on account of these and it was suggested that, at moderate cost, a shelter might be erected in front of the meeting house so that all might be seated and protected in case of rainy weather'.

This was agreed and the 'verandah' was put up in the following year. It does little for the beauty of the place but has been of service to those attending ever since. In 1877 it was reported that 200-250 people had attended. The minutes referred to it as a 'public meeting'; but the locals called it 'Gooseberry Sunday'.

From 1855 until 1920, or later, there were two meetings each Armscote Sunday. (As noted in Chapter 5, there was an allowed meeting at Armscote in 1913-14.) In 1917, QM was worried about a 'threshing meeting' with harmonium and hymns, but this does not seem to have been repeated. The Salvation Army were there for some years but we do not know if they brought their band. About 30%-50% of those attending then were said to be Friends and that the morning meeting was after the manner of Friends; the afternoon one was too, at least in theory, but one gets the impression it was somewhat mission-orientated. In that year QM noted that a Friend from London had been at Armscote General Meeting 40 times in 41 years.

A report to QM in 1920 said:

'The attendance was the largest for several years, Friends being present from Birmingham, Coventry, Evesham, Sibford, London and other meetings. The meetings were held under the guidance of the Holy Spirit and [were] a time of help and blessing. An open-air meeting was held in the village between the morning and afternoon meetings. Through the kindness of our Friend W. B. Gibbins, tea and mineral waters were provided'.

Armscote General Meeting continued until 1980 when the fabric of the meeting house was judged to be unsafe. For a few years 'Armscote Sunday' was celebrated at the nearby meeting house at Ettington, still on the first Sunday in August, but the meeting was able to be held again at Armscote from 1989. In that year the meeting house was full with about 85 people present and, as in the past, with Friends from quite a wide area. Tea was provided – under the verandah – but there was no 'tent-lunch' for Friends, as had been provided by W. B. Gibbins for some years up to 1914.

Armscote General Meeting has an unusual history and, today, there is nothing quite like it in London Yearly Meeting. It is not easy to say why the phenomenon of a once-a-year General Meeting has survived so long, attracting people (by no means all of them Friends) from a wide area. But it has clearly been worthwhile.

Campden becomes Broad Campden (1656 to 1991)

The history of Campden Meeting in the 17th-19th centuries, and its re-creation as Broad Campden in the 20th century after 88 years of closure, is also of some interest. It has a claim to be regarded as one of the oldest – some would say the oldest – meeting house in use in Britain, if not in the world.

The date when Friends first met at Campden is usually given as 1657 but a record has recently been discovered of a birth there in 1656 and that can now be taken as the earliest date known. A burial took place there in 1661, the infant son of William and Honor Dark (probably) of Weston Subedge; and there was a marriage there in 1662 between John Morris and Margery Sambage. In 1663 Friends bought 'two bays of housing and an orchard' for use as a meeting house and burial ground from John and Prudence Hitchman who were Quakers. (A 'bay of housing' was the distance between the principal upright timbers along the line of a house – usually 16ft. The smallest cottage would be 'one bay' and that was also the normal stabling space for two pairs of oxen – the oxen used to plough the mediaeval open fields.)

The Hitchmans also owned the adjoining land to the south, and a cottage (now called 'Box Cottage') was built there in the same year, 1663, and the Hitchmans presumably moved into it. They had, almost certainly, lived in the 'two bays of housing' prior to 1663 and it seems, though it cannot be proved, that Friends had had meetings in their house for some time (the reference is to 'our hired house') and, perhaps, from 1656. The building was clearly already of some age in 1663 and it has timbers of uncertain age and provenance which are older than the building. The meeting house provided at Broad Campden was the first non-conformist building in Campden (which term covers both Chipping Campden and Broad Campden).

The size of the meeting house was increased by half (to 'three bays of housing') in 1677, the main reason for this being the need to provide accommodation for the women to have their own business meeting. A loft was incorporated (the roof seems to have been raised to allow for this) and shutters were provided – these could be closed to allow men to have their business meeting in the meeting room, and women to have theirs in the loft. Or the women could have met downstairs under the loft. In any event, the loft would have been necessary when many people used the meeting house, for example when QM was held there. Pine panelling was introduced but none of it remains apart from the front of the loft and part of the small stand in the meeting room. Building was completed in 1735 when stables were provided; all that remains of these today is a flight of stone steps up to (presumably) a hay loft and these are just over the wall (in the garden of Maidenwell) adjoining the north wall of the meeting house.

The first trustees were Edward Warner, a weaver of Blockley; two Thomas Kites, elder and younger, who lived in Broad Campden, of a family of landowners thereabouts; Thomas Mosely a husbandman; William Dark a glover and John Morris a milliner. The Warner family are still represented at Blockley and there are many of the name of Keyte (as it is now usually spelt) in the neighbourhood, as well as Hitchmans (from whom the meeting house was bought) and Haydons (several early trustees bore that name). As noted earlier, William Warner, a brother of Edward, went to Philadelphia and the name of the suburb of Blockley there is said to originate with him. Other prominent Quaker family names in the 18th century included Bevingtons (clockmakers and tanners), Corks (who farmed at Charingworth), Ashbys (of Sezincote and elsewhere), Hemmings, Jephcotts, Gilkes and Gilletts – names still found in our area.

Sufferings of those at Campden have been noted earlier – see pages 32 and 43.

Campden and Stow MM was set up in 1668 and consisted of only the two meetings. Stow did not have a burial ground until early in the 18th century and presumably used the one at Campden until then. We have records of early burials at Campden (from the Public Record Office in London) but in many cases it is not possible to say which came from Stow and which from Campden. The MM was part of Gloucestershire QM and their minutes show that both Campden and Stow were not strong in the early days. In the 1670s, QM made several payments 'for the poor in Campden'; and contributions from Campden and Stow to QM were small or non-existent. In 1698 QM decided that 'an epistle be sent to Campden and Stow to stir them, especially to keep their Monthly Meetings together and also to attend QM more often'. Not much improvement seems to have taken place and they were prodded again in 1730. But by the mid-18th century both meetings were sending contributions to QM and also appointing representatives to go there – other smaller meetings were doing far worse at that time. QM was held at Campden twice in the 18th century but did not visit Stow. The MM was laid down in 1790 when it combined with Shipston MM and Warwickshire South MM to make an enlarged Warwickshire South MM.

Many books which refer to Campden mention Jonathan Hull, the first patentee (in 1753) of a system to propel a boat by steam; it was tried out on the Avon at Evesham but it failed. He is said to have been a Quaker, and to be buried at Campden Meeting's burial ground, but searches locally, at Friends House in London, and at the Public Record Office in London, have provided no confirmation. He undoubtedly existed and lived at Broad Campden ('Hulls House' still exists), but may or may not have been a Quaker.

Campden was never a large meeting and seems to have declined in the 18th century, and more so in the 19th, the main cause doubtless being rural depopulation. The men's and women's meetings were combined in 1812; shortly afterwards repairs to the meeting house were needed but were deferred as the number of Friends was small. The Government census of all places of worship one Sunday in 1841 included information about the capacity of the buildings. The Campden return was made by George Gillett of Brailes and he put the seating capacity at 300 in the meeting room and another 80 in the loft. This was, clearly, an over-estimate but it does pose the question – what seats were provided and how close were they together? Perhaps it was not very relevant on that Sunday as only four were present – and that may have included George Gillett. In 1851, when there were said to be only three Friends at Campden 'Who are very peculiarly circumstanced', the PM was brought under Shipston PM. MM last met at Campden in 1871 and the last burial seems to have been in 1872. The meeting was discontinued in 1874 'Owing to dearth of members'.

During the next 60 years the building was used part-time by various people; Friends always retained the right to hold meetings there but there is no evidence that they ever did so. A Blockley Evangelist used it for some years as did the Vicar of Campden and Primitive Methodists and, later, the Baptists. Sale was considered as 'there was no possibility of [its] being used by our Society'. The stables and some land were sold in 1889 but the meeting house was retained and even repaired. The land sold seems to have been 'Angel meadow', but the reference is not to the sanctity of Quakers but to a former inn. This was almost certainly an extension of the present burial ground to the east. This land, and the site of the stables, now form parts of the garden of Maidenwell.

However, Quaker activity in the area did not cease and there is information of meetings in Chipping Campden Town Hall in the 19th century and in a room behind 'The Gables' in the High St. in the first decade of the 20th century. Ephraim Webb of the latter meeting is said to have spent much time in trying to dissuade people from entering the (many) inns in Campden at that time. In 1917 Mr. and Mrs. C. R. Ashbee of Broad Campden (he had founded the Campden Guild in 1900) wanted to run a school in the old meeting house at Broad Campden but the scheme came to nothing. It was used for a Village Club for a few years from 1921 and was 'very much appreciated by the young men of the village'.

In 1931 Friends sold the meeting house and burial ground to the owner of Maidenwell; there was talk of it becoming a village hall but this did not happen. It was used as a barn for a time and American and British soldiers (the Green Howards) were billeted there in the 1939-45 war. They seem to have used the panelling over the stand to hang a dart-board – the many small holes there are not caused by woodworm. By the 1950s it was quite derelict and local people were worried that it was in danger of falling down; the local authority inspected it and a demolition order was issued. However, before anything could be done, Charles and Madge Tyson came (in 1957) from Lincolnshire to live in Chipping Campden. Charles was very knowledgeable about old Cotswold buildings and was a dedicated Quaker, so the old building fascinated him and he thought it right that it should be reconstructed and Campden become an active meeting once more.

There was an allowed meeting at Blockley three miles away which then had about eight members and attenders. Charles Tyson sought their support for his project but they were undecided. He then took the project to Gloucester and Nailsworth MM – the MM under which, according to Quaker rules of the time, any meeting at Broad Campden would fall. The MM was not in favour of the project; it was pointed out, reasonably enough, that the building was derelict and would need much money and effort to rebuild it and there was no certainty that a meeting would ever flourish there. So Charles took the matter to Warwickshire MM (which in 1937 had taken over Warwickshire South MM of which Campden Meeting had once been a part); Joseph Pickvance recalls that Charles was 'a very persistent person' and 'knew what he had to do' to retain 'this "gem" of Cotswold architecture'.

However, Warwickshire MM were not convinced either, though they agreed to set up a 'watching committee' to keep the matter under review.

The committee met a number of times as they recognised that the matter was urgent because the building might be demolished at any time; and some of its members also met individual Gloucester and Nailsworth Friends who were interested. After a time, some of them decided to try and buy the property. The owner of Maidenwell was approached and kindly agreed to sell it back for £100 – which the building had been sold for 30 years before. The conveyance was in 1960 and contained a special clause; it said that, if ever the building ceased to be a Friends Meeting House, the vendor could require that it be sold back for £100; but this option could not be exercised after the expiration of 21 years from the death of the last surviving issue of the late King George V.

Trustees were appointed and got the demolition order withdrawn; they made the building safe though it was still in a very bad state. There was a great crack in the north wall; the doors had gone (the entrances being closed off with bits of wood); the roof was in a bad state; the stone floor and the gravestones had disappeared; and the inside was chaotic with plaster from the walls over everything. Plans to rebuild were made and the matter bought back to both Warwickshire MM and Gloucester and Nailsworth MM. As the building had been bought and plans made, they agreed that an appeal be launched; it brought in about £3,500 which, in those days, was sufficient to bring the building back into use.

It was decided to restore it so that it was as nearly as possible as it had been in the 17th century. The only changes in the original lay-out (as far as was known) were that there were two doors instead of one from the lobby into the meeting room; all plaster was removed from the walls; a window was built in the south wall of what is now the kitchen; and the shutters between the meeting room and the lobby were made to open – it was thought this would allow a seating capacity of about 80. Of course, 20th century requirements had also to be met – a kitchen, lavatories, central heating – but this was done as unobtrusively as possible. And Banbury and Cirencester Meetings provided old Quaker benches.

The meeting house was opened in 1962, under the name of Broad Campden, with three members and three attenders (from Blockley). In 1991 there were 44 members, 20 adult attenders and 20 children on the list; and up to three-quarters of all these attend reasonably regularly. Providing for an increased number of children was a problem and in 1987 a 'garden room', a cedar-wood building which blends well with the Cotswold stone, was erected in the burial ground.

Broad Campden Meeting House is thus very much as it was in the 17th century and the meeting is a stable one. One might claim that it is probably the oldest meeting house in use; but it was 're-created' after 88 years of closure and dereliction. Thus it had not been in continuous use since the 17th century as, for example, Hertford Meeting House which has been used since 1670. So no special claim will be made for the meeting house, except that its history is remarkable and that it is a beautiful and peaceful place.

Sibford School

The Friends' School, at Sibford Ferris, was established in 1842 arising out of a concern which Joseph John Gurney and John Pease took to YM. Several QMs (Berks and Oxon leading) bought what is now the Manor House together with barns and a farmyard to provide the nucleus. The aim was to provide a good education for the children of Friends who had been disowned for marrying-out, but the school was open to all. It was (still is) run by a committee consisting only of Friends; and was to 'Afford a plain, useful, guarded, religious and moral education with board, lodging and clothing for children both male and female'. Boys and girls were together only for instruction but, in time, the school became fully co-educational like most Friends' schools. Initially there were 26 boys and 22 girls; the boys farmed the school's 25 acres and the girls helped on the domestic side, but this practice was discontinued in 1880. Many children came from afar – 'afar' might be only Northampton but it could take one and a half days travel. Because of the difficulties of travel, many children only went home once a year (usually four weeks at Christmas) but some with homes further away might be at the school for three years without a visit home.

The first 'Superintendent' was Richard Routh who filled that post for 38 years (1842-1880). He had at least one apprentice to assist him, indentured for five years to be taught the profession of a schoolmaster. The school developed under Routh's leadership and, among other things, the meeting house at Sibford Gower was rebuilt by Friends (in 1864) to allow attendance of the schoolchildren. After Routh retired, there were only three Headmasters in the 76 years to 1956 – four over a period of 114 years. In the 34 years since 1956, there have been another four Headmasters; one wonders whether the shorter tenure in this century is due to additional stress or to other factors.

The school has grown over the years from its small beginnings (but, unusually, it had a swimming pool from 1853) and now has 220 boys and 120 girls, of whom about 75% are boarders (these figures include the junior school opened in 1989); 8% of the pupils are children of Friends and about 5% of the staff are Friends. The school tries to ensure that every child has a real personal success – in academic or in City & Guilds subjects, in music, in the arts or in a combination of these. For those who show signs of dyslexia,

BROAD CAMPDEN

there is a centre which has won respect for its work. Every pupil is encouraged to give of his or her best so that a genuine sense of fulfilment and self-esteem can be developed. Success is not measured in terms of the curriculum alone; rather it is seen in individual terms wherever it occurs – in or out of the classroom. Music and drama are much in evidence and the range of sports is being augmented by a new sports centre.

The sixth-form provides for those who hesitate to take the traditional three 'A' level courses, because they may prove unsuitable and inculcate a sense of failure and disillusionment. All follow a programme leading to the Certificate of Pre-Vocational Education which might involve one or two 'A' levels and, in addition, courses in a number of other subjects. These might, for example, be Retail and Distribution, Horticulture, Care in the Community or Catering. Each pupil has his or her own timetable covering all the subjects involved, together with a three week period of work-experience locally. And all follow various 'core' subjects such as the use of keyboards and computers – skills which are essential today.

Those who wish to take a full three-subject 'A' level course are helped to take this at another Friends' school. Conversely, those from other schools come to Sibford so as to take the sixth-form pre-vocational courses. This is because Sibford has become nationally recognised for their pioneering work in such education. Friends have always been concerned to develop educational practice, as new needs arise, and Sibford carries on that tradition.

A particular feature of the school has always been the Sibford Old Scholars Association (SOSA). As early as 1904, 40-50 old scholars came 'from all parts of the United Kingdom, cycling and trudging along muddy lanes' with carts containing tents and clothing for a long week-end. They visited a number of local meetings and had lectures from well-known Friends as well as playing tennis and a cricket match against the school. Today there are about 500 in SOSA, in many parts of the world, and they still come to Sibford in large numbers. SOSA also gives financial and other support to the school and is an influential and wide-awake body.

Those who know Sibford School testify that it is a singularly happy place; indeed, the writer knows children who were positively anxious to get back to school at the end of the holidays.

East House (sheltered housing)

Another development has been in sheltered housing for elderly people. In 1968 Peter Scott spoke to Banbury and Sibford Friends of his vision of a 'community where the retired and elderly could live their own lives but could share common interests and pursuits as they desired – and could, when health failed, be cared for in their last illness so that all worry about their personal future could be removed'. As a consequence, and with the support of Berks and Oxon GM, a property – East House – was purchased in Adderbury East on the Aynho Road, and the Bray d'Oyly Housing Association was formed. (Bray d'Oyly was, of course, prominent in Adderbury Meeting in the 17th century.) In 1970 the coach house was adapted as a home for Peter and Richenda Scott while the rest of the project took shape. The square stone house was altered and extended to give single and double self-contained flats, together with a communal sitting room, a dining room and a warden's flat. The first residents arrived in October 1973; not all were members of the Society of Friends and this pattern has continued.

Peter Scott's vision of three types of accommodation, with an increasing amount of care, has not materialised as having several independent bungalows and a nursing home proved too expensive. But East House provides a midday meal every day, leaving the residents to make other meals in their own kitchens. With additions and alterations, East House now has 14 residents in three double and eight single flats. In 1989 adjacent land, belonging to the Housing Association, was let on a long lease to the Katharine House Hospice organisation (not connected with Friends). Their new building is expected to be complete in 1991 and to provide for terminally ill patients. It is hoped that the two communities will establish a close working relationship.

CHAPTER 5

The Evangelical Surge
(Attention is drawn to the warning in the first full paragraph of page 10)

For Friends, the biggest social issues in Britain in the last 150 years have probably been the disasters of two World Wars and many other conflicts, with the poverty and disruption which followed; the aftermath of the Industrial Revolution with its impact on social problems and poverty; and the flowering of the evangelical movement. By the late 19th century, when these factors were felt increasingly, Friends were in a better position to respond to new challenges because of the thorough revision of their rules and practices and because, as other dissenters, they had become free to hold public office and go to univesities. In our area the response to the evangelical challenge, which produced the adult school, Sunday school and mission movements, was of considerable importance.

In 1895, there was a Friends' Conference at Manchester. It considered the life and work of the Society and sought to discern new guidelines for the 20th century. The main conclusions were that more needed to be done to study Quaker origins and to work on Biblical criticism; and that summer schools should be encouraged to study these and other matters. The first summer school was in 1897, when over 600 Friends attended, and there were many more after that as QMs and MMs developed the idea. An important outcome was the setting up of Woodbrooke College in Birmingham in 1903 – the first of the Selly Oak Colleges there. It started with the study of religion generally, Biblical criticism and Quaker history and development, but widened in scope as time went by. Today it is a thriving body arranging the study (in Birmingham or out in the field with MMs etc.) of a wide range of religious and social subjects.

Looking back, it may be true to say that the Manchester Conference, and its aftermath, strengthened the desire to study Quaker and other religious history, and tended to turn Friends away from the more fundamental aspects of the evangelical movement. The Bible remained of

83

importance but there were those who thought it not infallible; and there was much less emphasis on, for example, sin and conversion.

The evangelical movement

The evangelical movement arose in the latter part of the 18th century and flourished in the 19th century – indeed it flourishes in many parts of the world today. It had many roots, one of which was the ministry of John Wesley and, by the end of the 19th century, the movement had virtually permeated all the churches. The way it was propagated by the nonconformist churches – bringing the message to high and low through low-cost voluntary organisation – was in itself pioneering. The effect on public opinion was dramatic and, among other things, forced governments to change from old-fashioned ways to reform in many fields. Indeed, the 'welfare state' of today can be regarded as a child of the evangelical movement.

It may be helpful to suggest a definition of what the word 'evangelical' meant 100 years ago. A conviction of personal sin; redemption of sin through the crucifixion of Jesus Christ; a strong belief in the Bible as God's word and an infallible guide to life; importance of family prayers; an impulse to expose the sins of the world; and a missionary zeal in bringing others to the same opinion through conversion. The fruits included a religious revival of a new kind; humanitarian attitudes which changed society; a new social conscience with an emphasis on education and temperance; and, above all, a new stress on the importance of the individual. Today one might add that with this went the attitude of some that the role of the poor was one of submission; and that some at least were quite antagonistic to the old established churches.

British Schools

British Schools originated at the beginning of the 19th century with Joseph Lancaster, a Quaker described by Ormerod Greenwood as 'A teacher of genius but [an] unpredictable man'. He ran a school at Borough Road, Southwark, on his 'monitorial system'. This system used older pupils to teach younger ones; the idea was not new, dating from at least the 16th century, but Lancaster embellished it and gave it new life. Out of his work there came the British and Foreign Schools Society (BFSS) which was Quaker-based but grew into a considerable organisation under royal patronage. The Quaker William Allen (a driving force in many fields of philanthropy) was much involved and the BFSS started British Schools in many towns in Britain, including Banbury and Evesham. As early as 1815, William Allen could claim that the French Government was setting up 12 schools in Paris, using Lancaster's methods, and that such schools were established in North America and at Calcutta.

The Borough Road College for Teachers was established near the school, which was then at Isleworth; and it was active until 1977. It was a basis for what has been described as the 'First world campaign for mass literacy'. Student teachers came to Isleworth from many countries in Europe, North and South America, Asia, Africa and Madagascar. The work may not be thought to have arisen directly from the evangelical movement, but it was consistent with that movement.

The Adult school, Sunday school and mission movements

The adult school movement came before the other movements and the first adult school was set up in Nottingham in 1798 by William Singleton and Joseph Fox (a Quaker). Initially, such schools were for the instruction of adults in reading and writing to enable them to read the Bible and become better people; then and subsequently, most were held early on Sunday mornings and they were often known as the 'Sabbath Schools'. As Friends increasingly saw the need for education in the country, they played a major part in the movement. In 1847 the Friends First Day School Association (known as the Double-F-DSA) was set up. It was a co-ordinating and stimulating body; initially, the emphasis was on children but later it became fully involved with adults too. By 1870 there were over 6,000 adults and juniors in the FFDSA field and, by 1900, the number was about 28,000 – so there were, then, far more attending Friends' Sunday and other schools than attended their meetings for worship.

The evangelical approach to the Bible, and the importance of temperance, were central issues and the pattern was that children started at Sunday school, went on to junior school and then to adult school. Activities were added progressively, the number depending on the size and strength of the particular school. There were savings banks; sickness benefit schemes; coal clubs; coffee carts (to sustain those at long sessions and also to provide a service at factory gates); concerts and indoor and outdoor games. In the larger towns there were clubs and institutes with reading rooms and other facilities. Birmingham was one of the first large towns to develop such activities and, later, they gave support to the work in our area and to Evesham and district in particular.

After the Education Acts of 1870 and 1885 the need changed somewhat as children learnt the 'three Rs' at school. However, many felt the need for further study when they left school and, in consequence, adult schools added to their curriculum both academic subjects and vocational training such as ambulance work, cooking, dressmaking and bee-keeping. In 1891 the National Council for Adult Schools was formed and about half the Council members were Quakers. The adult education movement developed and after 1914-18 the Worker's Education Association (WEA) emerged; and it flourishes today.

It is not surprising that, with much evangelically-based teaching, the mission movement blossomed. Mission meetings (often called 'Gospel meetings') were started in many meeting houses from the 1880s onwards. They met the needs of many – particularly those who had been to adult schools – who wished to belong to some religious organisation. The meetings consisted of Bible readings, hymns, extempory prayers and short prepared addresses – and harmoniums were much in demand. The emphasis was on personal salvation but physical, moral and intellectual well-being was also fostered.

Many meetings adapted existing accommodation to provide for the new activities and in many large towns (and also around Evesham) new buildings were erected. There were cottage meetings (winter) and tent meetings (summer), gospel vans and the like. Many Friends were slow to adopt these innovations; this is perhaps understandable as most Friends had known nothing but unprogrammed meetings, mostly in silence, all their lives. A Home Mission Committee was set up in 1882 but many Friends were hostile to it until it was reconstituted by YM in 1894. A main aim in all this work was the spread of temperance. 'Bands of Hope' helped children and young people to recognise the dangers of alcohol and they were encouraged to 'sign the pledge'; and the message was brought to adults too. The social background to this was that consumption of alcohol had been rapidly increasing during the industrial revolution and was blighting the lives of many of the poor; and the rapidly increasing number of public houses offered social activity as a lure. 'Christian Endeavour' was also of importance as it aimed to inculcate thrift and good housekeeping in young people; and Samuel Smiles *Self-help* was a much-used book.

Generally speaking, Quaker work in these fields came later in our rural area than in the large towns. In Yorkshire, for example, the peak in the adult school movement seems to have come in the 1880s whereas, with us, the peak was around 1900. But everywhere these movements helped to change the Society of Friends and its outlook. In 1899 John Wilhelm Rowntree thought that the adult school movement was the most important Quaker work in the previous 100 years, and it seems clear that most Friends were shaken out of any inward-looking lethargy and became accustomed to working with other organisations. The benefits of the shake-up are still to be seen. Perhaps we are now in need of a new shake-up and another crusade?

For attendance at mission meetings in our area see page 69.

Evesham and District

The most considerable mission work was in and around Evesham; minutes show interest in both mission and temperance work from 1877 and the first decisive action was in the early 1880s. Evesham Friends started a mission meeting on Sunday evenings, in place of the evening meeting for worship, and there was soon another on a weekday evening. The response was good and a Bible class, together with adult and children's school, was established in 1883/4. An early leader of the movement was Alfred W. Brown (author of *Evesham Friends in the Olden Time*); he was a recorded minister, who preached in the streets of Evesham, but died in 1891 at the early age of 32. In 1891 George Ash, seconded by the Home Mission Committee, came from Gloucester to lead the work. Cottage and tent-meetings, and some adult schools, were started in the villages of Cleeve Prior, Littleton, Badsey, Aldington, Harvington, Broadway, Ashton-under-Hill and elsewhere.

In 1892-4 the meeting house at Evesham was altered and enlarged to deal with the new work. William W. Brown built the 'Cowl Street Hall' in memory of his son Alfred W. Brown; (it is thought this is the, now derelict, brick building on the far side of the small car park immediately adjoining the meeting house to the north). Apart from the villages mentioned above, there were mission meetings and some adult school work in Pershore which is thought to have been run from Evesham but might have been the responsibility of Worcester.

By the mid-1880s Evesham had added a class for young women; a mixed adult class for Bible study and another for juveniles; weekday evening classes; mother's meetings; prayer meetings; a Sunday afternoon class for the children of members, later extended to any children; and an adult school at the Commercial Road Hall with another at the British School. MM was 'much struck with the unity and brotherly kindness which appears to prevail amongst them. There is a very general conviction of the truth of the views of Friends'. In 1890 Evesham PM noted that adult school and mission work was on 'strictly unsectarian lines' and that they endeavoured to promote 'physical, moral and intellectual as well as spiritual well-being'.

In the 1890s Evesham PM heard from a group of people who had been meeting for worship in a little room at Littleton, asking to come into fellowship with Friends. Evesham Friends gladly agreed and were supported in this by MM. Similar action was taken, later, with Badsey. Thus Evesham did not create Littleton and Badsey (though individual Evesham Friends were involved from an early stage) but took them under their wing. It was the start of a long period of co-operation and joint action. Western QM's view was that 'it is only at Evesham [within the QM] that Christian and philanthropic work can be reported and carried out exclusively by members of our Society' and that at Evesham 'aggressive Christian work has been carried out by Friends and made its mark for God in the neighbourhood'.

Work at Evesham around 1900 seems to have been:

Sundays
Morning meeting for worship
Children's Bible class
Adult Bible class for newcomers
Prayer meeting
Evening mission meeting
Sunday schools for men,
   women and children

Weekdays
Mission meeting
Young Friends' Union
Women's meeting
Men's class
Reading meeting
Band of Hope
Christian Endeavour
History and principles of Friends
Gospel meetings (with
   Littleton and Badsey)

Other work included the visiting of the sick (one Friend worked whole time on this – it seems mainly Bible reading); special missions to, for example, pea pickers; occasional missions lasting several days; and special temperance meetings – these, and some other work, being run jointly with other non-conformist churches. Clearly a lot of effort went into all this, typified by George Ash's work schedule for a Sunday in December 1892; from Evesham to Harvington for 8.15 adult school; back to Evesham for morning meeting for worship; at Badsey in the afternoon for adult and children's schools; an evening mission meeting at Littleton and back to Evesham – 19 miles on foot in winter.

Our information is not complete but by 1912 only three considerable activities are reported – Sunday morning meeting for worship (about 20-25 present), Sunday evening mission (about 40-60 present) and the children's school in three grades. However, teacher training classes (for Sunday schools) had started (probably) in conjunction with Littleton and Badsey. During the 1914-18 war, the work continued to decline but there was new work supporting conscientious objectors and helping German prisoners of war. The mission meetings seem to have ended by about 1923 and after that there were only meetings for worship and children's classes.

Badsey

Adult school work started in Badsey early in 1891 and was taken up by George Ash and others later that year; at Badsey the emphasis was on adult school work more than mission. Thirty students were on the register in 1891 and there were 165 at a school tea in 1892. (Judging by the reports, the size of the school tea was a measure of success in those days.) However, the accommodation was unsatisfactory and it was decided to construct a new building. William W. Brown and Henry Burlingham, both of Evesham Meeting, were large contributors to the cost but money came from Friends all over the country. Badsey Adult School and Mission Room was opened (300 to tea) in 1894; it was the only non-conformist place of worship in the village. Like Littleton (built later) it was in red brick in the Victorian style. Badsey became part of the MM in 1899 and had its own PM from 1910. The accommodation included the adult school room (which could seat 184 to tea), a classroom for 30, a library and a caretaker's cottage. The schoolroom originally had a large stand with lectern but later it was changed to what is in effect a pulpit (as at Littleton) known as 'The Rostrum'. The rostrum could be removed to make a stage for concerts etc.

In the summer of 1899 there was an 'anniversary meeting' and this became an annual fixture for a number of years. Of the first one a minute said 'It was felt by all at the meeting that there was a divine overshadowing and that [the speaker] was helped in his service to minister so that his labours were not in vain in the Lord'. Attendance was good – 160 to tea – and in the evening 'Dr. Sessions gave solos' and pieces were 'learned and rendered' by the children 'which gave much satisfaction'. Dr. Philip(?) Sessions was an Evesham General Practitioner and his name only appears briefly in the records; but there is an oral tradition which says that he was of great help and support, to Littleton as well as Badsey, on adult school and much other work.

By 1900 there were also two agricultural missions and lantern exhibitions on temperance (admission 1d). There was, unusually for Friends (but Badsey and Littleton were different) a meeting on Christmas Day as well as a children's party a few days later. There was an annual harvest festival and annual outings for children, e.g. by wagon to Broadway. But money was a continual problem and there was penny-pinching as well as fundraising activities such as sales of work. This was not just for running all the activities but for work in the village which was a particular care. During a measles epidemic and other sickness in the village 'a very earnest desire is manifest in this committee, and prayerfully laid before the Lord, for a greater measure of blessing on the village'. And 'systematic attempts were made to reach those who do not go to any place of worship on Sunday nights, as being as much in need as those sick in body'.

In the period 1900-1914 the pattern of the main regular events seems to have been as shown below. The numbers in brackets against some items indicate the numbers said to have been active on them in 1907 and 1912; these figures do not come from a national census (Chapter 4) but are local estimates.

– Meeting for worship on Sunday morning (30 in 1907 and 70 [half children] in 1912).
– Sunday evening mission meeting (100 in 1907 and 100-150 in 1912).
– Children's Sunday schools/scripture classes (100 in 1907 and 134 in 1912).
– Adult school Sunday afternoon (55 in 1907 and 30-35 in 1912).
– Women's meetings week-day afternoons (55 in 1907).
– Band of Hope, week-day evening in alternative weeks (100 in 1907).
– Bible class, week-day evening (25 in 1907).
– Christian Endeavour (30 in 1907).
– Missionary Helpers Union (fortnightly). (Overseas mission work was the subject.)
– Service of song with Littleton choir.
– Benevolent Committee ('Much cheer and help has been rendered').
– Tract distribution and general visiting.

THE EVANGELICAL SURGE 91

There was an annual mission week but little information on it is available. Of the 1903 mission week it was said 'The attendance was good and there was an earnest spirit throughout. We believe that much good was done, particularly among believers, but regret that few unsaved were known to decide for Christ'.

When Badsey had its own PM in 1910 it began to deal with business in a more Quakerly way and send representatives to MM. But, like Littleton, the minutes were different from most meetings; for example using the term 'Sunday' and not 'First day' and using titles such as 'Mr'. and 'Mrs'. Clearly it was not quite as most other meetings – but worthwhile. A visitor in 1910 wrote 'I never attended Badsey Meeting for worship without getting a spiritual uplift; it really is a most inspiring meeting . . . and about a third of them are teachers in the Sunday school'.

It seems that activities began to decline before 1914 and this continued in the 1914-18 war and afterwards. One gets the impression that less was attempted and fewer attended, and by 1939 Evesham was being asked to support them as their numbers were few. In the 1939-45 war the building was used as an evacuee centre (the meeting asked that 'no Catholics or Jews, preferably non-conformists, will be sent') but some meetings continued. Things did not recover after the war and in 1950 the meeting was discontinued. It restarted as an allowed meeting in 1955 and had a harvest festival in 1956. The Friends Evangelical Union carried out some mission work there in 1961 but it did not last and Badsey was finally discontinued in 1962. The building was sold in 1979.

Littleton

Mission meetings were held at Littleton from the early 1880s organised by a shoemaker called William Bentley; at Littleton the emphasis was always on mission more than adult school work. Meetings were first held in a cottage and then in the 'Co-op upper room' one evening a week. The room was supposed to hold 50-60 people but held twice that number at times – it got so hot that the paraffin lamps are said to have gone out because of lack of oxygen. From the early 1890s these meetings were run for Friends by George Ash and Thomas Bubb. The 'Friends Mission Room' – it always was called 'The Room' – was built in 1896 with contributions from some 60 Friends from all over the country; but the people of Littleton paid for the land it was built on. It was independent to start with, came under Evesham Meeting in 1896 and had its own PM in 1904. The building consisted of a large meeting room (seating 120) with a movable rostrum as at Badsey. Behind the meeting room was a class room and committee room (used today by a children's play-group) together with a kitchen etc. In 1897 20 men and women applied to the MM for membership – all in one letter – and all were accepted into membership together.

It is difficult to describe the activities in The Room as there were many developments and changes, but the 1900-1912 pattern was broadly as follows:–

Sunday
– Meeting for worship – said to be mostly men (about 30 attending in 1905 and 120 in 1912).
– Sunday schools for men and women. Sometimes joint men and women (about 40 in 1905).
– Sunday school for children (about 70 in 1905).
– Evening mission meeting (about 130-150 in 1905 and 80-100 in 1912).
– Bible class.

Weekdays
– Women's meeting (later called women's fellowship) grew to over 100.
– Band of Hope, more than 100 children.
– Girl's class.
– Mission meeting.
– Young people's club.
– Young men's mission.
– Bible class.
– Christian Endeavour.

There was a brass band which started about 1910. It led an open-air meeting on many Sundays and then marched to The Room for the evening mission service at which it also played. The 1914-18 war reduced its activity but it did not close until the 1930s. There were many outside activities such as tract distribution and visiting the sick and poor. For much of its life, The Room was used every night of the week, except Saturdays when it was cleaned and prepared for the Sunday.

There were also annual events:–

– Sunday school 'anniversary' on Whit Sunday afternoon and evening.
– Children's Sunday school concert. This was in the autumn and raised money for Christmas presents for the children.
– Children's Sunday school party on Boxing Day. It seems to have faded out in the 1914-18 war.
– Good Friday. Tea in the afternoon (later abandoned). Orchestral and vocal music from local choirs and those from other villages; later called 'cantata' as one was sung. There would be a Gospel story or other reading in the interval.

- Open air service on Littleton Hill on the first Sunday in August with the brass band as well as other bands from the district. Many would attend; on one occasion there were said to have been 400-500.
- General Meeting. This was on a week-end each summer starting in 1933, but there appear to have been similar occasions from time to time before that. There was a Quaker speaker from outside the area (usually a well-known one – the Cadbury family and Birmingham Friends were particularly helpful) and the aim was stated to be to 'publish truth and provide spiritual fellowship'. On the Sunday morning there were the usual arrangements specially augmented.
- Harvest festival on a Sunday in September or October. Meeting for worship in the morning followed by a service with a speaker; children in the afternoon; sale of produce on the Monday.

There were periodic 'socials' and concerts for adults (music was always a feature at Littleton) and, in the 1920s and 1930s, coffee mornings to raise money for specific charities. A monthly newsletter ran from the 1920s until 1950. As at Badsey, money was usually short and there were sales of work to raise funds. The Room was used by other organisations, such as the Salvation Army, but it seems that no charge was made. However, money could be found when really needed and in 1915 a building was acquired (about 200 yards west of The Room) as a club room. The Young People's Club had met in The Room since 1898 but more space was required; it was then possible to expand the activity to include young people from further away. Drinking, smoking and gambling were not allowed but games such as table-tennis and billiards were encouraged. In the early days it had about 40 members and met five nights a week; but it declined in the 1930s and the building was sold in 1939.

There was a slow decline in the 1914-18 war and between the wars, not so much in the activities as in numbers attending. The 1939-45 war brought new problems with evacuees using The Room; and there were reductions in the Sunday school numbers as some parents did not like Quaker pacifism, and also because many children became 'rowdy', closing it for a while. There was a guild of youth (which may have partly filled any vacuum left by the closure of the club room); and there was work with German prisoners of war. After the war there was further decline, particularly in the evening meetings, but the women's fellowship still had attendances of around 60. United Tent Meetings were held with other denominations and there were visits from the Caravan Mission to Village Children. For a year or two, evening classes were run in The Room by Birmingham University.

The Band of Hope and the men's weekday meetings ceased in the 1940s; the Sunday school, girl's classes, guild of youth and women's fellowship meetings ended in the 1950s; the concerts continued until about 1950; the General Meeting was dropped in 1960; the Good Friday services ceased in 1980; and meeting for worship was held twice a month from 1983 and once a month from 1985; and in 1985 the PM was discontinued and the meeting merged with Evesham. Now (1991) there remains the meeting for worship on third Sundays and the fellowship meeting held every Sunday evening, with about 12 present of whom, perhaps, only two or three are Friends. There are only a handful of Quaker mission-type meetings left in the country, two others being at Hartshill and Stirchley not far to the north of our area.

The Vale of Evesham as a whole

The rise and decline of the Vale of Evesham mission and other work can be judged from the following estimates of average annual numbers (taken from QM minutes). Information for attenders was not available for the latter years and figures for them were always somewhat uncertain.

Year	Evesham Mem	Evesham Att	Badsey Mem	Badsey Att	Littleton Mem	Littleton Att	Total of All 3 meetings Members & Attenders
1885	33	4	–	–	–	–	37
1890	47	5	–	–	–	–	52
1895	63	70	–	–	–	–	133
1900	79	99	9	75	20	91	373
1905	83	30	16	70	21	85	305
1910	78	5	31	35	27	38	214
1915	69	8	34	38	25	41	215
1920	48	3	28	20	31	39	169
1925	38	N/A	39	N/A	31	N/A	N/A
1930	42	N/A	33	N/A	30	N/A	N/A
1935	44	N/A	27	N/A	25	N/A	N/A
	In 1990 meeting for worship and children's class only. 33 members excluding Littleton		Discontinued in 1950 but an allowed Meeting 1955-1962.		In 1990 meeting for worship once a month. Fellowship meeting every Sunday evening. In effect, three members (part of Evesham).		

In the YM proceedings of 1902 it was recorded that 'Evesham with Badsey and Littleton may well be glad that 700-800 persons are influenced directly by the agencies of Friends – and many more indirectly by visitation'.

The Home Mission Committee's representatives facilitating work at Evesham, Badsey and Littleton were:-

George Ash	1891-1905. (He and his wife, Maria, retired to live in the district about 1920.)
Mark Lawson }	In two separate periods covering 1905-1917
Charles H. Siddle }	approximately.
Asher Davidson	1909-1917.
Richard H. Smith	(and his wife Mildred) 1920-1931. However, he did not work full time for Friends as he had probation and hospital work as well.

From, in particular, 1917 onwards important roles were played by Arthur E. Thorne (at Evesham), Walter Stewart (at Badsey) and Thomas Bubb (at Littleton – his son Frederick followed him). They all had long been involved in the work but they had their own employments (mostly market gardening) and there was a limit to what time they could devote to Friends' work. Thomas Bubb was the grandfather of Philip Bayliss now of Littleton and Evesham Meetings.

Shipston and district

In 1885, Shipston PM was a small weak meeting with two meetings for worship a week. By 1888 they had begun to move into the mission field and, at their request, the Friends Home Mission Committee provided the assistance of George Wood. It was not long before there was a gospel meeting on Sunday evenings and it is said that the many newcomers looked upon the meeting house as their regular place of worship. An adult school was started, failed and was reopened in 1890 on a weekday evening. There was also a young women's Bible class, a Sunday school for children, mother's meeting and children's meeting and, later, a men's Bible class. In 1891 Shipston Friends said that

> 'Though feeling our weakness it has seemed right to take on one branch of work after another, trusting that strength will be given us. We thankfully acknowledge that we have been helped . . . in so an unexpected manner that, instead of depression, our hearts have been filled with praise and thanksgiving'.

In the late 1890s two women (not Friends) were employed (the QM paying the costs) to visit the sick and infirm in and around the town – as Shipston Friends were not able to do this work. About 25 people attended young men's Bible classes and another 25 the adult school on weekday evenings. A young men's club was set up in 1897, a girl's sewing class in the same year, with a Band of Hope in 1902. Cottage meetings were held at Tredington and Willington, and a temperance society was set up at Shipston and another (with Band of Hope) at Burmington. In 1894 it was decided to establish 'preliminary membership' for those attending these activities who were not Friends, and they were formed into a 'Friends Christian Society'. However, only eight joined and the scheme seems to have lapsed when YM's proposal to have 'associate membership' for such people was not generally accepted in our area.

In about 1902 W. B. Gibbins, of Ettington Meeting, bought a cottage at Blackwell, had it pulled down and replaced it by a hall for the use of the village as a religious centre. Friends ran a mission meeting there from about that time; it was held twice on Sundays and was mostly attended by old people who had no other place of worship. An allowed meeting was held there from 1916 until about 1919 and all Quaker work in the hall seems to have ceased at about that time. A children's class was started in 1919 (not in the hall); it is not known how long it continued, but it went on until at least 1923.

In 1904 Abraham and Katherine Harris came to Shipston from the Home Mission Committee and remained until 1908; they returned in 1914 and remained until 1928. Christopher Lawson was the Committee's representative from 1912 to 1915. Among other things he started an allowed meeting at Armscote which lasted almost two years, collapsing when he left. He returned to the district in 1919, having a business at Ettington, and worked with Friends in various ways.

In 1915 a recreation ground was provided for the village of Shipston and this seems to have been largely paid for by Friends; it was opened by W. B. Gibbins of Ettington Meeting. It was well used and was handed over to the local authority to run. About the same time a mothers' meeting was started at Tredington, and it was said there was not space for all who wanted to attend. A coal club was started and socials were established in the Shipston meeting house schoolroom. By this time the men's school on Sunday mornings had an attendance of about 40 and the women's on Sunday afternoons of about 38. However, numbers seem to have started to fall because of the 1914-18 war and the summer outing (apparently an annual fixture) was cancelled; but a room was made available for wounded soldiers for games and other recreations and there was also a mission for them.

By the early 1920s the Shipston mission meeting had around 60 attenders and most other activities seem to have been continuing. The adult school had 118 names and 'had a very important place in the town' with at least some of the work in outlying villages continuing. Young men were given vocational training (at Shipston) on such things as bee-keeping and 'the wireless' and there was a summer open-air meeting held with other denominations. The decline is not well recorded but by 1930 there were two meetings for worship on Sunday at Shipston, another mid-week and a mission meeting; but no mention of anything else. In 1956 Shipston meeting as a whole was discontinued.

North Oxfordshire Generally

Banbury MM (Banbury and Sibford were then the only meetings of any size) decided in 1891 against having any paid staff on adult school and mission work. Thus, unlike the Worcestershire and Warwickshire Meetings, there were no Home Mission Committee staff resident in the area. There was a Banbury and Sibford Friends Library and Tract Association which flourished for many years. QM was not in favour of those at mission meetings being invited to be 'associate members', as proposed by YM, but Banbury PM, backed by the MM, appointed three from the Neithrop Mission (see below); but the idea does not seem to have been taken any further.

Sibford

A children's class was started in 1870. The first mission meeting was in the early 1880s and, prior to that Joshua Lamb says, Sibford Friends looked on even the small children's class with suspicion as being a 'creaturely activity'. (This was regarded as being activity decided upon by people and not action arising through the inspiration of the Holy Spirit.) A mission room was acquired in 1879 together with a room for the Band of Hope and other work. By 1882 there was an adult school for young men on two weekday evenings, and social gatherings were started for Friends and those attending adult schools and mission meetings. By 1885 a 'reading meeting' was started in the meeting house. A Friend would read from a Quaker book or other suitable material and, thereafter, the meeting would be wholly or largely unprogrammed. These reading meetings were held in the winter months only and were partly for the benefit of those attending Sibford School. As recorded in Friends Book of Meetings, they only lasted a few years; however, Joshua Lamb says they continued until about 1930 and it seems probable that their nature changed from time to time.

By the 1890s there were added mission meetings on Sundays (also called 'gospel meetings') with many villagers attending; new Band of Hope and temperance work; another adult school on Sundays; Sunday classes for young girls; a men's Bible class on weekdays and another on Sunday (about 16 attending); a mother's meeting in winter (with 22 on the books); a

Missionary Helpers' Union in conjunction with Sibford School; religious instruction for young people; prayer meetings; together with a savings bank and a sick-fund. There was also temperance work, Bible classes and the like in Friends' houses in Sibford and in nearby villages.

In the early 1900s there were (including those from Sibford School) 74 members and 64 non-members on the Sibford list. There were by then two children's classes on Sundays (for different age-groups) and talks (for the school) on Quaker principles. There was a branch of the British Women's Temperance Association with 26 members. The adult Sunday school had about 45 on its books with an average attendance of some 27. By 1914 the only activity we can be certain of was the two meetings for worship on Sundays (the evening one being a reading meeting or the equivalent) with a children's Sunday school and a Sunday Bible class. However, there are indications that there were, in the 1914-18 war and in the early 1920s, periodic gospel meetings or prayer meetings.

During the 1939-45 war, the mission room housed two families of evacuees from London and the meeting house was also used to extend the village school. After the war the only activity, apart from meetings for worship and children's classes, seems to have been a 'Bright Hour' (hymns, a prayer and tea for women) on a weekday which continued until about 1980. This was in the mission room which was, and still is, used for various purposes both by the village and by Friends.

Banbury

There was work by Friends on temperance in particular in Banbury in the mid-19th century. See page 57.

In 1875 there was a centenary procession of Sunday school children of all denominations in Banbury. There were 61 children of the Society of Friends and 160 from the Neithrop Mission. The number of non-conformists was given as 494 and the total for all churches as 3,059.

Some of the adult school, Sunday school and mission work carried out by Friends was done in the buildings of other organisations, in addition to work done at the meeting house in the Horsefair. A Temperance Hall was opened (not by Friends) in 1875 at the junction of Bridge Street and Mill Lane. It was primarily used by the Free Mission for Evangelical Work but the Plymouth Brethren were there for a time. Banbury Friends started using it in 1883. It was purchased by a trust (80% of the money is said to have been contributed by Friends) and in 1895 it became the Cadbury Memorial Hall named after James Cadbury. James Cadbury was an outstanding local Quaker. He first worked as a grocer but later was engaged in insurance, perhaps to give more time for his voluntary work. He was much involved in temperance work and with the allotment movement, and was active in the British Schools, the Bible Society, the Board of Health and the Mutual Aid Society. The purpose of the Cadbury Memorial Hall was, again, to promote temperance and it was laid down in its constitution that it was not to be used for 'Proclaiming principles opposed to Christianity (Old and New Testaments)'. Banbury Meeting was not responsible for it but most of the trustees were Friends; four were Gilletts and all four bankers.

Neithrop was, in the late 19th century, a rather disreputable part of Banbury with a large workhouse. In 1868 a cottage was acquired for inter-denominational use (it is not clear whether Friends used it) and, in 1873, the Banbury Sunday School Union built the Neithrop Mission Hall at the junction of Warwick Road and Neithrop Avenue. The brick building still stands, though now derelict, and it is said that there was, beside it, a 'tin hut'; Friends later did much work at Neithrop but it is not known if it was all in the brick building or all or partly in the tin hut (which no longer stands). Friends started to use the Neithrop Mission in 1901 when it was described as 'disused'.

It should be said that in all mission, adult school and Sunday school work in Banbury at the turn of the century – Quaker and otherwise – the Gilletts, Braithwaites, and Cadburys had wide influence. William Charles Braithwaite (the author of those splendid books *The Beginnings of Quakerism* and *The Second Period of Quakerism*), who died in 1922, was a partner of Gilletts Bank at Banbury. He was not only active in temperance work and Quaker Meetings but ran an adult school for men at the Windmill, a converted inn at 56, North Bar (near the Horsefair Meeting House) used for non-Quaker temperance work, missions and adult schools. His two sisters, Rachel and Catherine, who came to Banbury in 1920 did much work inside and outside the Society of Friends. They were strict evangelicals and teetotallers and, for example, would not cook any food on Sundays. After the 1914-18 war, Lizzie and Lottie Brown were very active – particularly in the provision of necessary refreshments. They sold Banbury cakes in the 'original cake shop' – they were related to Samuel Beezley who started the business.

The pattern of work at Banbury is hard to ascertain or describe and it seems best to try and indicate what the position probably was in 1905 – which may have been the peak year. Reference is made to Cherwell and Grimsbury; these are parts of Banbury but it is not known where Friends' work there was carried out and it seems likely that it did not last there for more than a few years. Some dates are given in brackets below (they indicate the first known date of a particular activity) and attendances are indicated where these are known.

Meetings for worship

Horsefair Meeting House	Sunday mornings Sunday evenings (but at some periods this may have been dropped as Friends converted it into a mission meeting) Weekday evenings
Cherwell Grimsbury }	Little known except that they were 'small'
Neithrop Mission	A PM minute said that meetings were 'as much after the manner of Friends as is practicable having regard to the minds and religious experience' of those attending. Neithrop had an allowed meeting 1909-1920. In 1917 a (Banbury) PM minute said 'The members of the Neithrop Mission are not definitely encouraged to join our Society because the Friends who conduct it believe that, at present, they are most suitably helped by means of the mission membership form of application which is as follows "Believing on the Lord Jesus Christ as a Personal Saviour it is my desire to become a member of your church"'.

Sunday schools

Children	Horsefair from 1875 or earlier. Neithrop from 1903; about 150 attended that year
Juniors	Horsefair
Young Friends	Horsefair from 1894 Neithrop
Adults	Temperance Hall/Cadbury Memorial Hall from 1883 Neithrop

Mission meetings

Men	Neithrop (from 1901)

THE EVANGELICAL SURGE

SHIPSTON-ON-STOUR — FROM AN OLD PHOTOGRAPH (C 1890)

Mixed	Horsefair from 1884
	Neithrop from 1903 (60-80 attended 1903)
Women	Cadbury Memorial Hall from 1895(?)
Adult schools (not possible to divide by sex)	Horsefair from 1884
	Neithrop from 1901 (30-40 attended 1903)
	Temperance Hall/Cadbury Memorial Hall from 1883(?)
	Cherwell
	Grimsbury
Bible class	
Adults	Horsefair from 1894
'Lads'	Neithrop
Women	Horsefair from 1894 (monthly)
Bible reading/study	Neithrop
	Horsefair (winter only)

Poor girls' sewing with religious and other instruction	Horsefair from 1891
Christian Endeavour	Horsefair from 1901 Neithrop from 1903
Missionary Helpers Union	Horsefair from 1885
Temperance (adults)	Cadbury Memorial Hall since 1895
Band of Hope	Horsefair from 1885
Mothers' Meetings	Horsefair from 1894
Socials etc.	Horsefair from 1885 Neithrop from 1903

Prayer Meetings were started later – about 1915.

It was reported in 1903 that about half of the Banbury Friends were involved in adult school, Sunday school and mission work. There were occasional Quaker Meetings in the Union Workhouse and Friends visited workhouses, hospitals, etc. There was individual work on temperance as well as on peace issues. Friends worked with a number of other organisations such as the YWCA, Girl's Help, Brother's Meetings and 'benevolent institutions'. There was reference to a Friends Temperance Band, probably based on Neithrop, but nothing is known about it.

The decline of this work is not well recorded but it seems to have largely disappeared in the 1914-18 war or soon after. In the 1939-45 war, eight old lady evacuees lived in the Horsefair Meeting House in a hostel looked after by Elizabeth Spurway and Hilda Davies, wardens acting for the Friends' Relief Service.

South Newington, Hook Norton and Adderbury

There was a small meeting at *South Newington* which was reopened in 1892 largely to allow weekly mission and temperance meetings; but there was also a fortnightly meeting for worship. It was said to be 'well attended by those in humble life who seem to appreciate these opportunities' and attendances of up to 60 are reported. A weekly Sunday school for adults was started in about 1901 and a women's meeting, monthly, a year or two later with about 18 present. There were lectures and social gatherings with up to

70 present. The meeting was discontinued in 1911 having been a part of Banbury Meeting and much supported by them as well as by Friends from Sibford. At about the same time there was mission and adult school work at *Hook Norton* which was part of Sibford Meeting. The work seems to have been partly in the meeting house and partly Friends' homes; it was probably on a small scale and does not seem to have lasted long. At *Adderbury* a Bible class was started in 1889, and an adult school and mission meeting both in 1891. In 1905 the mission meeting was described as a 'threshing meeting' with 50 present. Adderbury was part of Banbury Meeting; as it had only three members it was much supported by Banbury Friends. The meeting was discontinued in 1910 and all activity ceased then except that a Bible class seems to have continued for a time.

Note on sources for this chapter

Much of the information in this chapter has been deduced from those PM, MM and QM minutes which are available. The word 'deduced' is used because minutes are a record of what was done at the meeting and do not normally record what was reported on, for example, adult school work. So one is collecting bits and pieces of information from more than one source. Apart from minutes, there is some published material for the Vale of Evesham (see Appendix 3) and, for Sibford, the unpublished memoirs of Joshua Lamb; it has also been possible to draw on the memories of a number of older people. There is difficulty in distinguishing between activities. How many separate activities are covered, for example, by 'Women's meeting'; 'Mothers' meeting'; 'Womens' fellowship'; 'Women's class'; 'Adult school for Women'; 'Women's Sunday school'; and 'Women's Bible class'? Such terms may have meant different things at different times, or been used in different ways by different people, so interpretation is difficult. It is hoped that what is given here is reasonably accurate, but there can be little certainty. The source material used has given a series of snapshots, many out of focus, rather than a continuing picture.

CHAPTER 6

Retrospect

Seed corn

We have considered the work and lives of Friends in our area over some 340 years. Here we look back at some points and start by looking again at Friends' work in the period 1700-1860 covered in Chapter 3.

Commercial work (clockmaking, plush weaving and banking) was reported in North Oxfordshire but little was said on what was done elsewhere. The explanation is that North Oxfordshire (in particular Banbury) was reasonably prosperous while other places suffered from depopulation and economic depression. However, it seems right to consider what Friends' interests were in the 17th and 18th centuries, outside earning their living and the ordinary running of their meetings. It is suggested that what they thought and did in the general humanitarian field was a necessary prelude to what Friends have been able to do in the last 150 years; that Quaker thought and effort in those times was the 'seed corn' of much Quaker work today.

Within meetings there was much emphasis on education and the care of children and young people. Every meeting contributed to Ackworth School in Yorkshire (run by YM) and, later, to Sibford and other schools. And post-education stages were also important:

> Banbury MM 1793. 'Theo Plester agrees to take Samuel Green apprentice as a linen weaver (and also a plush weaver if he can entitle him to that trade) for seven years and to find him clothing and all necessities for that period – having with him a clear premium of 12 guineas; to which this meeting agrees providing his mother is unable to do so, or in some part thereof, herself.'

A tangled story on the care of children comes from Warwickshire South MM in 1792. William Harris seems to have gone to the West

Indies and disappeared. The meeting sent two of his children to Ackworth School and the third was to go to her grandmother if her mother agreed; it was implied that, if the mother did not agree, Friends might withhold assistance. The mother did not agree to the child going – but Friends sent this child to Ackworth just the same. Eventually, the mother was disowned for 'acting very unbecoming in giving her company to men' and the child went to the grandmother.

Banbury MM 1800. 'John Walford being returned from Ackworth School, and being in need of a situation, this meeting desires [two friends to] provide for him in the best manner they can at present, and endeavour to find a place for him.'

Banbury MM 1819. 'The cashier is directed to pay another year's bill of admission for Hannah Bright at Islington Road School, her father agreeing to advance £4 thereof.' (Islington Road School, in London, was later at Croydon. Today it is at Saffron Walden.)

Our meetings supported The Retreat at York (an early Quaker mental hospital) on a regular basis even though only a few from our area went there. Then there were those who fell on hard times for one reason or another:

Oxfordshire QM 1687. 'Simon Hawkins of Banbury complains to the meeting that he has sustained a great loss by fire and it was ordered that he be paid £5, Banbury MM paying half the amount.' In 1748 Banbury MM had a special collection for a Friend who had lost 'six of seven cows due to distemper'.

Warwickshire South MM 1800. 'Mary Ashby having applied to us for assistance, it is agreed to allow her three shillings a week . . . In order to discharge this, and other expenses, it is earnestly recommended that those Friends who are of ability will make a more liberal contribution.' Or the same MM four years later 'John Palmer and his wife, being grown in years, and his sight very indifferent, the meeting appoints . . . to pay them a visit to see if they want any assistance'. At the following meeting it was agreed to assist them.

While Friends took much responsibility for their members, the trust was mutual. In Warwickshire South MM in 1792, a Friend who, for a considerable time had had financial assistance from the meeting 'having a legacy left him by a distant relation he hath . . . honourably refunded Friends . . . what they had advanced'.

Friends outside the area were helped too. Even in the early days there were, for example, special collections for Friends imprisoned by Turks or by Algerian pirates. There was a special collection in 1738 for 'Friends in difficulty in North America'. And Friends, and also Mennonites, were given assistance to emigrate to America. There was much concern about slavery and Friends examined their own consciences on the subject – 'Due enquiries have been made from house to house by Friends appointed; Friends appear to be free respecting the slave trade' (Warwickshire South MM 1768). In 1835 there was help for coloured people in North Carolina to move to slave-free states; and later for 'freed people of colour in North America'. Assistance was provided for North American Indians and for the education of negroes in the West Indian Colonies. There were protests against the Zulu wars, the opium traffic in China and the supply of alcohol and arms to Africa. Nearer home, in 1746, there were collections for 'those suffering after the late rebellion in Scotland'.

Quaker relief and development work grew gradually over the years. To start with the work was done by individuals who gave freely of their time, but most had their own livelihoods to earn and could not be away for more than a few months. As the work increased, they came to be supported by committees at home which raised money and gave limited support – for example, various 'War Victims' Committees'. Emphasis was at first on food, medicines and other relief to enable people to survive; later tools and the like were provided to help people rebuild their lives. Such principles are followed today by Oxfam (which has some Quaker orientation) and other development agencies. Action was taken to relieve suffering (on either side) in the Napoleonic wars, the Crimean war and in the Franco-Prussian war. There was work in France, the Netherlands, Poland and Russia during and after the First World War; and work was on an even wider scale in the Second World War. Starting in the 1860s the Friends Foreign Mission Association worked in Africa, Madagascar, Ceylon, India and China with emphasis on medical work and educational (often higher educational) study. All or much of this work received the moral and financial support of those in our area.

Since 1914, the scale and urgency of the need has resulted in increased Quaker effort both in Quaker organisations and by individual Quakers working elsewhere. Bertha Bracey, late of Banbury Meeting, who died in 1989 aged 95 years, is perhaps the best remembered of those in our area who did such work. She was involved in helping Germany with its problems in the 1920s and, in the 1930s, with helping Jews and others to leave Germany and settle elsewhere. One could go on describing such work – but most Friends are aware of the many activities of our Society.

However, these activities did not come into existence over-night. The Holy Spirit has inspired Friends to do such work and it has grown up steadily over many years. The work started in the 17th and 18th centuries when Friends were brought to see what was right, and how to act; and act they did despite local poverty. We must not forget that they laid down the paths which we, their heirs and descendants, now try to follow.

From the minutes

Reading minutes one is struck by some traditional Quaker phrases used repeatedly; the wording was not always the same but the formula was. For example:

- Someone being accepted into membership, 'deserving the notice of this meeting'.
- Visitors were recorded as 'We have with us the very acceptable company of . . .'
- 'After due enquiries having been made it would appear that . . .' was a favourite.
- On someone wanting to make a religious visit elsewhere, the formula was 'Our dear Friend hath laid before us a concern which has long rested weightedly on his/her mind to . ...'
- Many things were 'solidly' or 'weightedly' considered. Influential Friends were 'weighty Friends'.
- Church rates (and other such abominations) usually had 'so called' in brackets after the description.
- In Banbury MM in the late 18th century a favoured phrase, often repeated, about needing money was 'It appears to this meeting that our cashier is considerably out of pocket and . . .'.
- Some clerks repeated a set formula of words in many minutes. For example, in Gloucestershire QM in the 17th century, the opening minute quite often was ' . . . where Friends are met together to serve the Lord his truth and people. And Friends are desired to take care that no disorderly persons sit in the meeting when business is entered upon; and such are chiefly intended hereby [are those] who have been disowned and not reinstated, and such who are under dealing and have not reformed to the satisfaction of their Monthly Meeting'.

In the 18th century in particular, YM and QMs spent much time in formulating rules and spiritual and other guidance. This came in YM minutes, epistles and other documents, and efforts were made to see that they were widely studied – often this was required twice – and a local minute even appointed a Friend to 'deliver a copy of the YM Epistle to each family, and also to see that it is read'. But YM did not only advise, it enquired into many things – such as how information was collected and how appointments were made. QMs were directed to consider whether meetings for worship were held 'at such hours as leave the body free from drowsiness'. (It is thought that, for much of the 18th century, meetings for worship were largely silent and lasted for about two hours.)

Warwickshire, Leicestershire and Rutland QM advised (in 1832) that 'when a minister kneels down in the solemn act of prayer . . . there would be propriety and advantage in Friends rising up without turning round'. (Standing up when prayer was offered in meeting continued until this century. It is said that, when Friends House was built in London in the 1920s, the seats in the large meeting house were spring-loaded so that they became vertical when people stood up. Many rising together made much noise, so the practice ceased at YM and, gradually thereafter, at other meetings.) Worcestershire QM 1754 'This meeting recommends to the several meetings to strictly examine whether any of their members have taken anything as reward for their vote in the last General Election. And if such appears, to deal therewith and report to the next QM'.

Both YMs (London and also Bristol – see below) and QMs issued queries and revised them periodically. QMs got reports from the MMs in order to draw up replies to YM; and MMs got reports from PMs, so as to compile their replies to QM. As an example, the queries by Warwickshire QM late in the 18th century were as follows:

1. Are meetings for worship and discipline [i.e. business] duly attended and do Friends avoid all unbecoming behaviour therein?
2. Are love and unity preserved amongst you? And do you discourage all tale-bearing and detraction?
3. Is it your care, by example and precept, to train up your children in Godly conversation and in frequent reading the Holy Scriptures; and also in plainness of speech, behaviour and apparel?
4. Do you bear a faithful Christian testimony against the receiving or paying of tithes, priests demands or those called church rates?
5. Are Friends careful to avoid all vain sports, places of diversion, gaming and all unnecessary frequenting of ale-houses, taverns, excess of drinking and intemperance of every kind?
6. Are Friends just in their dealings and punctual in fulfilling their engagements?
7. Is early care taken to advise and deal with such as appear inclinable to marry contrary to the rules of our Society? And do no Friends remove from, or into, your monthly meeting . . . without certificate?

8. Have you two or more faithful Friends deputed in each particular meeting to have an oversight thereof and is care taken, when anything appears amiss, [for] rules of our discipline to be put in practice?
9. How are the poor among you provided for and what care is taken for the education of their offspring?
10. Doth any person of your meeting travel as a ministering Friend that is not in unity with you?
11. Do you keep a record in your MM of the prosecutions and sufferings of your respective members? Is due care taken to register all marriages, births and burials? Are the titles of your meeting houses, burial grounds etc. duly preserved and recorded? And are all legacies and donations properly secured, carefully recorded and duly applied?
12. Are there Friends of your meeting in want of apprenticeships or servants likely to be supplied from Ackworth School?

Queries had to be answered regularly and much time was taken in considering reports and drawing up answers. Naturally, there was a certain sameness and caution about the replies. As an example, some of the answers to queries made in 1800 by Warwickshire South MM were:

– 'We fear there is not much growth in truth among us; some little appearance of convincement hath appeared since last year.'
– 'We believe that Friends are at present in a good degree of love towards each other; if differences arise care is taken to endeavour to end them speedily and we hope Friends are careful to avoid and discourage talebearing and detraction.'
– 'Friends who have children and servants under their care, we believe, endeavour to train them up in religious life and conversation consistent with our Christian profession.'
– 'The Holy Scriptures are frequently read in our families; and mostly [Friends] keep to plainness of speech, behaviour and apparels.'
– 'None of our members receive or pay tithes, priests' demands . . . and church rates – that we know of.'
– 'The necessities of the poor amongst us are, we believe, faithfully inspected and received: and good care is taken in the education of their offspring.'

Those who act as doorkeepers today may wish to reflect on guidance given in 1699 'They are to attend the meeting house doors to hinder all rude people from troubling the meeting'.

The Bristol Yearly Meeting and its Circular Meeting

Circular Meetings arose in the north of England early in the Society's life and flourished in various places. They were for the benefit of those in an area, the venue moved around and, broadly speaking, they were for worship only and not for church affairs. They were not significant in our area until the 18th century.

Besides the Yearly Meeting in London, there was established in 1695 a Yearly Meeting in Bristol to which certain QMs sent representatives and whose queries they answered; Worcestershire and Gloucestershire QMs were involved but not Warwickshire and Oxfordshire QMs. It was recognised that the Bristol Yearly Meeting was additional to, and not in place of, London Yearly Meeting. Besides its administrative responsibilities, it was an occasion when Friends travelling in the ministry could meet together and when meetings for worship open to the public were held. The Bristol Yearly Meeting's importance diminished as the Circular Yearly Meeting of the Western Counties grew in importance. It might be added that both London Yearly Meeting and Bristol Yearly Meeting were sometimes referred to as 'annual' meetings.

The Circular Yearly Meeting of the Western Counties was started in 1720 at the suggestion of Bristol Yearly Meeting. The meeting moved about within Worcestershire and Gloucestershire, within our area, and from 1774 within Warwickshire also. The Circular Meeting met each autumn at places as far apart as Exeter, Taunton, Barnstaple, Hereford, Kidderminster, Coventry, Gloucester and Helston. In towns where there was no suitable hall, a 'booth' was erected. One such was at Evesham in 1771 when the cost of the booth was £56 (being paid for by the surrounding MM and QMs) and another was at Shipston in 1784 when again a booth was built. A Circular Meeting usually lasted three days, in which time there would probably be two select meetings (for ministers, elders and perhaps other Friends) and four public meetings. There were many non-Friends attending including those 'called the "quality", the gentry and several national priests'; and also 'high professors of religion' and a 'mixed multitude of all sorts and notions'. Overflow meetings often had to be held and ministers 'preached to great multitudes', up to 4,000 being mentioned for one meeting. Many of those attending held religious meetings in the towns and villages they passed through going there and returning.

At a meeting of Bristol Yearly Meeting, with the various QMs involved, in 1787 the state of the Circular Meeting:

'Having come under our solid consideration, we are of the judgement that, though it has been pretty largely attended by those

not of our Society, the number of representatives from the counties, and other solid Friends, have been few; and for the most part the sittings thereof have been laborious and very exercising . . .'
The Circular Meeting was then dropped; and Bristol Yearly Meeting itself was discontinued in 1798.

Visits

There were various types of visits. There were visits to all meetings by travelling ministers, of which there is little record, and also religious visits made by particular Friends to a locality, which were usually recorded. A redoubtable visitor of the second type was Sarah Lamley of Warwickshire South MM. In the spring of 1811 she was given a travelling minute (certificate) by her MM which was recorded in full in the minutes and is typical of many such.

'To the Friends in the Quarterly Meetings and Monthly Meetings in the counties of Kent, Sussex and Surrey. Dear Friends, our beloved Friend Sarah Lamley hath laid before us a concern, which hath long rested weightedly on her mind, to pay you a religious visit, both in your particular meetings and families, and requested our concurrence; and also that she might have liberty to appoint meetings, among those not in profession with us, as truth may open the way in the course of the visit – and also in going and returning. Which, having been solidly considered by us, we hereby inform you that we have good unity with her as a member and a minister in her present concern. Hoping that she may be favoured to perform the visit to your satisfaction and comfort and to the relief and satisfaction of her own mind. With the salutations of love we are your affectionate Friends'. (Signed by 15 women and 17 men).

The certificate was returned in the following autumn 'she having been enabled to perform the visit to the peace and satisfaction of her own mind and, we trust, the comfort and encouragement of those among whom her lot has been to labour'. Sarah Lamley died in 1836 and the testimony to her life said:

'From the year 1790 to 1823 she visited, with certificates, we believe all the Quarterly Meetings in England and Wales with the exception of six or seven . . . From 1823 to 1833 she visited many of the meetings in her own Quarterly Meeting and also held many public meetings – such was the abundance of her labours, and the devotedness of her heart to the cause in which she was engaged, that we feel incompetent to do justice to her character'.

Religious visits were also made overseas, and overseas Friends came here. Three examples from Banbury MM:–

In 1756 'James Taylor having heretofore acquainted this meeting of his concern to visit Friends in America, the same has been weightedly considered and as he hath now intimated . . . it still rests on his mind. It seems to be the sense of this meeting . . . that he should be at liberty to proceed on his religious visits as way may open thereunto, and that a certificate be prepared for this purpose . . . And, as it seems necessary that enquiries be made into his outward circumstances in order to making suitable provision for the assistance of his family during his absence, [names] are desired to make enquiry and report what they think necessary to be done thereon'. At the next meeting it was reported that 'he hath therewith to satisfy his creditors and to supply his occasions for the present'. A certificate 'liberating him to travel' was issued. Over two years later he returned his certificate to MM and 'gave an account of his witness into America which was to good satisfaction; and likewise he produced several certificates from Friends in divers places of his good service and becoming deportment'.

A visit of a different kind took place in 1883. 'Charles E. Gillett, a member of this meeting, is intending to accompany his uncle and cousin, J. B. and W. C. Braithwaite, together with the Secretary of the British and Foreign Bible Society, on a visit to some of their depots in Eastern Europe and Asia – and also to the meetings of Friends in Constantinople, Brummana and Ramallah'. He was given a travelling minute, and had another such minute in 1886 when he made a similar journey. (Brummana and Ramallah were mountain villages, near Beirut and Jerusalem respectively, where Quaker work had been started).

1895. 'We have at this time the acceptable company of our Friend Rufus P. King, of North Carolina, with a minute of Springfield MM, Deep River QM, North Carolina YM, liberating him for religious service within the compass of London and Dublin Yearly Meetings.'

Another kind of visit was when a MM sent Friends on a special visit to a local meeting. A minute of Warwickshire South MM in 1807:

'It appearing to us, in answers from Campden particular meeting, that a breach in love and unity is existing among a few Friends there and, it being desirable to resolve the cause if possible, we appoint [Friends] to pay the individuals a visit'. Two months later it was reported that those who visited 'took an early opportunity with them and had considerable satisfaction therein and entertain a hope that the time when a thorough reconciliation will take place is at no great distance'. In 1808 it was reported that 'breach now completely healed'.

An interesting example of how a meeting's answers to the set 'queries' brought action from the MM and a successful visit.

A kind of visit, different again, was when YM sent a committee to visit some local meetings to consider organisation of the religious life there. A report in 1761 read:–

'Dear Friends, in the course of our religious visit to the MMs in this county [Warwickshire QM] we found that meetings for ministers and elders are duly held, though not a sufficient number of elders are appointed in each meeting. The appearance of all concerned as ministers is not so acceptable to Friends as could be desired and, indeed, it is to be found that some are too often prompted by a forward disposition without being properly baptised for that weighty work. And the elders have not discharged themselves towards such as they ought to have done. Harmonious labour seems neglected, there being a folding up of hands to rest which we desire may be again unfolded and they engaged in living service to the church . . . Drowsiness in meetings for worship is too prevalent in many owing to an indolent state of mind, void of that awful fervency which always attends the worshipping of God in spirit and truth . . . There appeared great deficiency in attending meetings for discipline and putting the rules thereof into practice. Friends are generally in love but true unity both in spirit and labour, we fear, [is] much wanting in many . . . And, dear Friends, as this visit sprang from a lively concern for the welfare of Zion and the enlargement of her borders we . . . entreat that you would arise from the state of supineness we fear too many of you have long remained in . . . but come into the Lord's vineyard and work, for indeed there remains much to be done therein . . .'

and so on at considerable length. This was not the only diatribe from a YM committee; and QM could be quite forceful too. But the tone became softer as the years passed.

Testimonies to the lives of those who have died

Testimonies to the grace of God as seen in the lives of deceased Friends were not frequent. Apart from that on George Fox, quoted at the end of

Chapter 2, they were about local people and were approved by MM and perhaps QM. They tended to be long but some were quite short and these give the impression that they were about somebody not very remarkable except that they were much loved. A few examples follow:–

1744. 'Elizabeth, the wife of William Bevington of Ettington did at several times appear in testimony in meetings, her ministry tended to excite Friends to seek after the profession and experimental enjoyment of which they profited. Often advising to guard against formality and empty professions, she visited divers of the adjacent meetings and was well received. She was a loving Friend and affectionate wife and, we hope, departed in peace on . . . and was buried at Ettington . . . in the 30th year of her age, a minister about seven years.' (Warwickshire QM)

1741. 'A short testimony concerning our dear deceased Friend Benjamin Kidd of Banbury who died at about the age of 59 and a minister about 38 years. He was a man much loved and esteemed not only by Friends but amongst his neighbours and by people in general of different ranks and persuasions. Naturally cheerful, and open and free in conversation, which rendered his company both profitable and very desirable, [he] being sound and deep in judgement and of great sincerity and integrity. A diligent attender at meetings and exemplary in his conduct amongst men. Eminently qualified by his supreme Dispenser of all good, for great and singular services in the church, not only in the discipline in which he was excellent and exhorted in great wisdom . . . Much might be said of his excellent qualifications and services and of the great loss we have sustained as well as the church in general . . . but we desire . . . that the great Lord, who so eminently filled and qualified him, [will] raise up many more such bright ornaments in the church so that Zion may become a beautiful habitation and Jerusalem the praise of the whole earth.' (Banbury MM)

Deborah Harris, widow of Long Compton. 'Her testimony was not large nor very frequent yet we felt it sprung from the pure foundation of life which made it wholly acceptable to the living amongst us; her life and conversation agreeing therewith. And having done her day's work, she hath left a good savour behind her. She departed this life and was buried at Long Compton . . . aged about 80 and a minister nearly 30 years.' (Warwickshire QM 1785)

Ann Ashby, born at Sezincote, Gloucestershire, in 1760 was an orphan and brought up by relations in Banbury with whose family she spent most of her life. 'It appears that divine love early visited her . . . and she was strengthened to take up the cross to her own will.' She became a recorded minister at the age of 34 and travelled much in the ministry both to families and to meetings. 'She was often led to speak instructively, and sometimes pointedly, to the state of individuals.' She was 'very affectionate in disposition . . . and on many occasions rendered important services to her friends in sickness'. In 1825 she left home and went to live with a family, where there was a serious illness, for some months; and she had to bury some of them. But her own health broke down with the fever she had been nursing. As she was dying of the fever she kept her friends away because of the danger. She died at the age of 66. (Banbury MM 1827)

We end this book with extracts from a testimony (Banbury MM 1864) to the grace of God as seen in the life of Joseph Lamb, a farmer of Sibford, who had been born there of Quaker parents in 1754.

'In his youth he had not the advantage of more than a very limited portion of school learning; possessed, however, of strong natural abilities which he perseveringly cultivated, he acquired a degree of self-instruction superior to many in his day . . . In his early life he was often visited with the Light which makes all things manifest and shows what the Lord requires at our hands. He appears, however, to have been too frequently disobedient to these visitations of his heavenly Father's love – to have indulged in some of the various amusements and vanities which do frequently beset the path of the young and, in consequence, to have brought himself condemnation. Still, however, the invitations of mercy followed him and we believe it was about his 24th year of his age that he became more decidedly serious and thoughtful respecting his external welfare.'

'He now began the attendance at weekday meetings to which he had not previously been accustomed and, although under discouragement from some outward sources, he felt much satisfaction in so doing.' In 1784 he was married to Margaret Hall of Hook Norton 'by whom he had numerous family'. They were married for 48 years until she died in 1832 'the recollections of her virtuous life, and sweetly peaceful close, is still fresh in the memory of her family and surviving Friends'.

'He believed himself called upon in the early part of the year 1791 to appear as a minister and he was so recorded in the following year. He was careful to train up his children to a diligent attendance of meetings and manifested much satisfaction when he saw any of them reading such books as instructed them in the truth of the Gospel . . . In meetings for discipline he was concerned faithfully to uphold the various testimonies of our Society; and the talents entrusted to him by divine grace rendered him a highly useful member.'

When about 70 he retired and lived on 'a small competency which he had been enabled, by persevering industry, to obtain'. He had, in time, much pain and lameness and was confined to home. When 82 he wrote 'Though I feel the infirmities, pains and weakness generally attendant on old age, yet I am mercifully favoured to feel peace and quietness both within and without. Oh, what a favour to be sensible to the life-giving presence of Him whom my soul loveth'. His final illness was short and he died in 1845 'upwards of 90 years of age and a minister about 53 years' and was buried at Sibford.

APPENDIX 1

Notes on Past and Present Meetings in our Area

INFORMATION IS GIVEN ABOUT each meeting in our area and some details are included which are not found elsewhere in the book, e.g. 'George Fox's table' at Adderbury. Some references are made to substantial material elsewhere in the book. For other items, please refer to the index.

QMs and MMs were set up in 1668 and, therefore, no earlier dates are given for them. QMs were all discontinued in 1966. For local meetings the date on which there is a first record of their existence is given – for example a marriage or a mention in a source such as George Fox's *Journal*. Thus, chance has determined what dates are available and various meetings may have been started earlier than recorded.

Some of the meetings listed are rather shadowy, e.g. Bishampton (21b below). They are known to have existed but few details about them have survived. Others may have existed, probably did, but we have no information about them.

(1) **Adderbury**
Banbury MM 1668-1910   Oxfordshire QM 1668-1790
                         Berks & Oxon QM 1790-1910
On entrance to graveyard in West Adderbury.
(OS grid ref: SP 465 354)
 The first report of a meeting there was in 1656.
 The present meeting house was built of local stone in 1675 by Bray d'Oyly, who was the Lord of the Manor. It is said to have been built on land he owned; he was certainly imprisoned for two months for being responsible for the building. The meeting house must be much as it was when built except that the stand is thought to be 18th century. It has an unusual and beautiful loft on three sides of the

meeting room. There was a small thatched house close by for the use of the women's meeting for church affairs; it was demolished in 1955. The burial ground is no longer in use but many headstones remain; some are made of iron.

George Fox is recorded as being there for the opening of the meeting house in 1675 and was there in 1673 and 1678; he was a friend of Bray d'Oyly and lodged overnight with him from time to time.

Apart from the meeting house and the cottage for the women, there were other buildings; a 'house' and a 'tenement' are mentioned. In 1755 the widow Jeffcot went to live in the tenement as she could not afford to pay a rent. An unspecified building there was sold in 1813 and a 'house' there was demolished in 1896.

In 1746 there were said to be 50 Quaker families at Adderbury, many of whom were clock makers.

In 1856 the men's and women's meetings for church affairs were merged because of the reduced state of the meeting. In 1861 the PM was discontinued and Adderbury came under Banbury; however, it seems to have had its PM restored at some date because in 1889 it was again placed with Banbury.

'The George Fox Table'. As noted above, George Fox is said to have been at the opening of Adderbury Meeting House in 1675; he will probably have sat at a gate-legged table of the Tudor period (which was probably given by Bray d'Oyly). The table remained in use at Adderbury until this century. After the meeting closed in 1910, Sophie Fanny Buck was allowed a key and worshipped there every Sunday. She continued with this until the 1939-45 war when there were evacuees in the meeting house; they used the table for kitchen work so Sophie took it into her house for safe keeping. When she died it was almost sold with her other effects, but local Quakers were able to recover it. At some stage in (probably) the 18th century a copy of the table was made for South Newington Meeting and was used there until that meeting was discontinued. The two tables are now preserved by Banbury and Sibford Friends and form a link with George Fox.

Sophie Fanny Buck died in 1945 and was interred in the burial ground at Adderbury where her grave can be seen. She not only had a meeting on her own in Adderbury for over 25 years but she often went there in Quaker dress.

The furniture which Sophie looked after also included two coffin stools. Some Adderbury Friends lived at Milton, a small village a mile to the west of the Adderbury Meeting House. When a Milton Friend died, it was usual to carry the coffin across the fields to the Adderbury burial ground. The coffin stools were used on these and other occasions. They too are preserved by Banbury and Sibford Friends.

The meeting was discontinued in 1910. The meeting house is still owned by Friends and there is a 'celebration' there, on the first Sunday of June, each year, which is attended by Friends from all over the MM.

A key to the meeting house is kept by the Warden of the Bray d'Oyly Housing Association's East House on the Aynho Road (A41).

(1a) There was an associated meeting at **Bloxham** two miles to the west (OS grid ref: (village) SP 430 358), Friends there being on the Adderbury list. The first record of a meeting was in 1665 in the house of George Ansen, a weaver. It seems never to have had a meeting house but had sufficient facilities (perhaps a barn) for MM to meet there from time to time. In 1774 William Harris had a meeting in his schoolhouse. The meeting was discontinued some time in the late 18th century.

(1b) Another associated meeting was at **Milcomb** ('Milcome') (OS grid ref: (village) SP 412 347) three miles to the west. The first report of a meeting there was in 1665 when Friends met in Edward Butcher's house. It is not known how long the meeting lasted but it had been discontinued by the late 1780s.

(2) **Alcester** ('Aulcester')

Redditch MM 1668-1706　　Worcestershire QM 1668-1790
Evesham MM 1706-1810　　Hereford & Worcestershire
Worcestershire MM 1810-1835　　QM 1790-1832
　　　　　　　　　　　　　　Hereford, Worcs & Wales
　　　　　　　　　　　　　　　*GM/QM 1832-1835
　　　　　　　　　　　　　　*Technically a GM. In effect
　　　　　　　　　　　　　　　a QM.

See page 33 for sufferings.

Established by Richard Hubberthorne in 1660. He was one of the Publishers of Truth from Yealand Redmayne in N. Lancashire.

The meeting house was built, and a burial ground provided (OS grid ref: SO 090 575), in 1677. It still exists at 28 High Street. It is now a private house and the entrance from the High Street is through a door, on the east side, between the Bear Inn and the Post Office. (At the time of writing, the shops on either side of the door are 'Alcester Electrics' and 'Alcester Locks and Do-it-Yourself'.) It is a squarish brick house which seems to have been altered many times. There are no gravestones in the garden but the present owner thinks that there were some over a wall in a yard used for commercial purposes. It may have been that the burial ground was partly in the garden and partly in this yard.

Viscountess Conway of Ragley Hall was a member of Alcester Meeting. She is known to have been generous to Friends and may have contributed to the cost of the meeting house.

In 1699 the meeting house was rebuilt. There was some connection with 'Kineton' – a fairly common place-name hereabouts. 'Kineton and Alcester' are mentioned in MM minutes. Sometimes Evesham MM was called 'Evesham and Alcester MM'.

In 1829 the meeting house was again rebuilt. In 1835 the meeting was discontinued and the meeting house turned into a dwelling house, and let.

In 1927 Worcester and Shropshire MM thought of selling it but, instead, Warwickshire North MM took a 21 year lease on the property. They thought it right to 'keep a foothole in Alcester for Quaker work' and hoped that it might become a meeting house again one day. They sublet it to a tenant who agreed that the (small) sitting room could be used for adult school work or a meeting once a week. It seems that it was used for both purposes for a number of years, but perhaps less frequently than once a week. In 1948 Warwickshire MM surrendered the lease and Worcester and Shropshire MM sold the property.

There was an additional burial ground at Cladswell, a few miles away, from 1784 until some time in the 19th century (see Ridgeway Meeting in item 21a of this appendix).

It is not clear why Alcester, which has always been in Warwickshire, was, from the early days, in Worcestershire QM and not in Warwickshire QM. It may be that Alcester followed nearby Shipston and Armscote Meetings which were in 'islands' of Worcestershire within Warwickshire. (Such 'islands' of Worcestershire were, until this century, in parts of both Warwickshire and

NOTES ON PAST AND PRESENT MEETINGS IN OUR AREA

Gloucestershire, their origin being that they were part of the lands of the mediaeval Abbey of Worcester).

(3) **Armscote** ('Armscott')
Dealing with Worcestershire QM direct 1668-1714.
Merged with Shipston 1714.
Allowed meeting 1913-14. Warwickshire South MM same dates.
Warwick, Leicester & Staffs QM same dates.

Armscote is one mile west of the A429 near Tredington. The meeting house is of local stone at the end of the village towards Tredington (OS grid ref: SP 246 448).

See page 70 for history of the meeting.

First record of a meeting there was in 1655; it merged with Shipston in 1714 and, technically, is a closed meeting. The meeting house and burial ground were provided in 1674-1705.

The Primitive Methodists rented the meeting house for their Sunday school 1863-1927 but this did not prevent 'Armscote Sunday' being held on the first Sunday in August each year. Extra land was bought to extend the burial ground in 1865.

An allowed meeting was set up in 1913-14 as part of Shipston Meeting. It seems to have been largely the creation of Christopher Lawson (who was the Home Mission Committee representative with Warwickshire South MM) and it did not long survive when he left the district.

The meeting house and burial ground are still owned by Friends and Armscote General Meeting is held on the first Sunday in August each year.

A key to the meeting house is held at Ettington Meeting House.

(3a) In 1685 there was a meeting at **Tredington** (OS grid ref: (village) SP 257 437). It is not known how long it lasted, but it was probably associated with Armscote.

(4) **Badsey**

Worcs & Shropshire MM   Western QM same dates.
1899-1962 (but closed 1950-1955)

Badsey Adult School and Mission Room, Chapel St. Badsey, three miles west of Evesham (OS grid ref: SP 072 432). A brick building now used by a school for dancing.

See pages 89 and 94 for history of the meeting.

First adult school work there was in 1891. The adult school and mission room was opened 1894. It became a recognised meeting in 1899 and had its own PM from 1910.

The meeting was discontinued in 1950 but reopened as an allowed meeting 1955. It was finally discontinued in 1962 and the building was sold in 1979.

(5) **Banbury**

Banbury MM 1668-1986 Oxfordshire QM 1668-1790
Banbury & Evesham MM Berks & Oxon QM 1790-1966
since 1986

Horsefair, Banbury (north-west of Banbury Cross). (OS grid ref: SP 454 406).

See pages 25 and 39 for sufferings.

See page 69 for attendance at meetings.

See pages 97 and 98 for adult school and mission work, the Neithrop Mission and the Cadbury Memorial Hall.

First record of a meeting there 1654.

The first meeting house was put up on the premises of James Wagstaff in 1657 – it seems to have been a temporary building as it was moved and re-erected on the present site in 1655; however it survived until 1750. In 1681 it was extended in some way to arrange for a room for the women's meeting. It is reported that in 1680 there were some 40 Quaker family names in the town.

The present meeting house was built in 1751 of local stone largely at the cost of Benjamin Kidd. It provided two meeting rooms. The larger has a considerable stand (with a row of seats in front as part of the structure) and also a large loft – though it appears this was built rather later. The room is now used by a children's play group. The small meeting room (once called the 'Women's meeting room') is used for meetings for worship.

The burial ground was extended in 1706 and 1814. In 1815 a 'garden' was added and it is now the paved area behind the meeting house. Among the last to be buried at Banbury were John and Ann

NOTES ON PAST AND PRESENT MEETINGS IN OUR AREA 123

Adkins who were the great, great, great, grandparents of Muriel Langley, now a member of Banbury Meeting. The last burial was in 1853.

In 1708 a school was opened in the meeting house run by a schoolmaster Timothy Spires; it was still going in 1723 with Friends paying part of the cost. In 1772 there was a 'teaching school' at the meeting house, but the subsequent history of this body or bodies is not known. In 1851 it was said that there were 'about 60 worshippers' at the Horsefair Meeting.

In 1906 a room was built at the end of the small meeting room for use as a schoolroom and also to help with the serving of meals when there was a visit from QM or any such body. It is now partly a store room and partly the women's lavatories.

The meeting house at Banbury remains in use but the burial ground is closed.

(5a) **Neithrop** (OS grid ref: SP 447 407) is a suburb of Banbury. Apart from the Neithrop Mission (see Chapter 5) there was an allowed meeting at the Neithrop Mission from 1909-1920.

(5b) The villages of **Tadmarton** and **Broughton** (OS grid refs: (villages) SP 394 397 and SP 421 383 respectively) are a few miles to the west of Banbury and both had meetings but it is not thought they ever had meeting houses. Both villages were under the shadow of Broughton Castle where Lord Saye and Sele was a powerful landlord and opposed the Quakers. It is not known how long the meetings lasted; they were associated with Banbury Meeting.

(6) **Barton**

Banbury MM 1668-1798   Oxfordshire QM 1668-1790
                        Berks & Oxon QM 1790-1798

Small rubble-stone meeting house and burial ground – 'Quaker Cottage' at the end of Jacob's Yard in Middle Barton (OS grid ref: SP 045 245).

It is thought that Friends first met there in 1668.

The meeting house was built or converted from a cottage either in 1668 or in 1700. It was always a small meeting but sent representatives to MM for quite a number of years. Originally, Adderbury burial ground was used but, later, Barton had one of their own. It declined slowly over a long period; it may have had a

PM at one time but there is no record of another meeting later becoming responsible for it.

In 1795 it was reported that the meeting was 'satisfactory' but, in 1798, MM appointed Friends to 'attend Barton Meeting and one of them is desired, at the close of it, to signify that the meeting is discontinued'. However, there were after this occasional meetings there from time to time, e.g. in 1809. The meeting house was let in the 1820s and finally sold in 1856.

There was a report of a meeting at nearby Steeple Barton in 1676 – but nothing else is known.

(6a) There was a meeting for a time in the 17th century at **Lower Heyford** (OS grid ref: (village) SP 048 244). It would have been associated with Barton or, perhaps, Bicester.

(7) **Bicester**

Banbury MM 1668-1790   Oxfordshire QM same dates

Always a small meeting and one which almost certainly did not have a meeting house. It was some way from the heart of the MM and rather isolated. (OS grid ref: (town) SP 058 223).

Earliest reference to a meeting there is in 1676.

In 1678 Friends were meeting in the houses of Edward Thomas and John Harper; and in 1697 they met 'regularly' in Harper's barn. However, this seems to have been discontinued because, in 1709, a 'new meeting' was set up by Jeremy Lepper (a labourer of Bicester) and William Giles (a wool merchant of Winslow) both of whom were heavily fined in 1708-9. In 1738 there were said to be six Quaker families in and near the town. A meeting room is said to have been off Sheep Street, opposite the 'Red Lion', but any building there has disappeared.

In 1749 John Griffiths of Philadelphia visited 'this small meeting' and found 'little of life or religion there'.

In the early days MM did not visit Bicester and contact seems to have been slight, Bicester sending representatives to MM only rarely. However, MM met there more than once in the 1780s and, in 1783, they called for a collection for Bicester who had not contributed to MM funds for some years. This may have been MM's last attempt to put new life into the meeting for, in 1786, it came under Adderbury for PM purposes and, in 1788, an MM minute said 'it is the unanimous opinion of this meeting that Bicester Meeting appears to be held to the disreputation of the Society'. In 1790 the few Friends remaining at Bicester were transferred to the Adderbury list and the meeting discontinued.

(8) **Blockley**

Gloucester & Nailsworth MM 1957-1962. Western QM same dates.

Four miles south of Chipping Campden where Friends met in the house of Frank and Jean Haine, 'Box Cottage' in the High Street. (OS grid ref: SP 165 347).

Recognised meeting (no PM) set up in 1957. Discontinued in 1962 when those attending transferred to the re-created meeting at Broad Campden.

(9) **Brailes** ('Brayles')

Warwickshire South MM 1668-1863 In early days sometimes called 'Brailes MM').
Oxfordshire QM 1668-1790   Berks & Oxon QM 1790-1863

Between Upper Brailes and Lower Brailes (at 'Cross Yeats Close') on the B4035 4 miles east of Shipston on Stour (OS grid ref: SP 307 394). The meeting house no longer exists.

See page 57 for plush industry.

First record of a meeting there was in 1657 when three Friends had goods distrained for non-payment of tithes.

Land for the meeting house was acquired in 1678 and building completed by 1686. A burial ground was provided and extended in 1705; but part of it was sold in 1860 as there was more space than was likely to be required.

In 1689 it was estimated that over 50 persons of all ages met at Brailes. In the 18th century numbers declined (emigration to America was particularly mentioned) and in 1738 meetings were only held monthly – but were back to weekly by 1760.

Early in the 19th century Friends were reluctant to spend money on repair of the meeting house as most members went to Shipston for PM and weekday meetings. The meeting was merged with Shipston in 1841. MM last met there in 1860.

The meeting was discontinued in 1863 and the building demolished (as unsafe) in 1869. The site was sold in 1891 and the Wesleyans built a house on the site for their minister. Later, permission was given for the minister and his wife to be buried in the Friends burial ground, and they were interred there in this century. It is a rather ornate marble gravestone with a kerb – rather different from the Quaker gravestones in local stone which only have initials and a date inscribed on them.

The burial ground is still owned by Friends but is disused.

(10) **Broadway**

Dealing direct with Worcestershire QM 1668-1717.
(Perhaps was 'Broadway MM')
To Evesham MM 1717. Was Broadway PM or perhaps merged Evesham PM.
Evesham MM 1717 to some date prior to 1750 when closed.
Worcestershire QM same dates.

Village on A44 seven miles south-east of Evesham (OS grid ref: SP 095 374).

First record of a meeting there was in 1662 – however, a Broadway Friend was fined at Chipping Campden in 1657 – see page 33.

Broadway Meeting sent representatives to Worcestershire QM in its own right until 1717 and tradition has it that there was a 'Broadway MM' with no other meeting; but this is not proven. It seems to have transferred to Evesham MM and merged with Evesham PM in 1717 (some sources give 1698 but it is thought 1717 is correct); but it might have had its own PM within Evesham MM.

The meeting was discontinued at some date prior to 1750.

No meeting house is known, but Friends owned a house with land there until it was sold in 1809. It might once have been a meeting house, but this can only be conjecture.

(11) **Campden/Broad Campden**

Campden & Stow MM 1668-1790
Gloucestershire QM 1668-1785
Glos & Wilts QM 1785-1790   } Campden Meeting
Warwickshire South MM 1790-1874
Warwicks, Leics & Rutland QM 1790-1854
Warwicks, Leics & Staff QM 1854-1874

Closed 1874-1962

Gloucestershire & Nailsworth MM 1962-1986
Western QM 1962-1966
Banbury & Evesham MM since 1986 } Broad Campden Meeting.

One mile south of Chipping Campden in Meeting House Lane, Broad Campden. (OS grid ref: SP 159 379).

See pages 32 and 43 for sufferings.

See page 74 for Campden's history and re-creation as Broad Campden meeting, after having been closed for 88 years.

First record of a meeting there 1656. Discontinued 1874 and re-opened 1962.

Meeting house continues in use. Burial ground disused.

(12) **Ettington** ('Eatington')

Warwickshire South MM 1668-1936	Warwickshire QM 1668-1790
Warwickshire MM 1936-1986	Warks, Leics & Rutland QM 1790-1854
Banbury & Evesham MM since 1986	Warks, Leics & Staffs QM 1854-1966

Old Halford Road, Ettington, six miles south-west of Stratford-on-Avon. (OS grid ref: SP 268 487).

See page 43 for sufferings.

The first record of a meeting there was in 1660 – said to have been in the house of Samuel Lucas who, in his will, left a 'little close' for a meeting house and burial ground.

The meeting house was built in 1684 and registered as a meeting in 1689. It is built of local stone with elm roof-timbers which appear older than the building. The lattice windows in the front appear to have Elizabethan catches and the very low door, heavily nailed and with a large boxlock, also appears older.

It is the smallest existing meeting house in the country. It has a stand which is unusual in that it is not on the wall facing the door. The stand is only six feet long and (as at Esher and Wallingford Meetings) is high off the ground – 17 inches at Ettington – which is the nearest approach to a pulpit in any early meeting house. There is an unusual dado of rush matting, thought to be 18th century, which was refurbished in 1986. The original meeting house had a stone roof but was slated in 1894. An extension (small room, kitchen and lavatory) was built in 1986.

Active meeting with a disused burial ground.

Note: In 1713 Stratford-on-Avon Meeting (Warwickshire Middle MM) agreed to join themselves to Ettington Meeting – perhaps for PM purposes only, as they seem to have continued to have a meeting once a month for a while. In 1732 they had a rented room but, in 1750-51, the meeting was discontinued and half the members (and half of the seats) were transferred to Ettington (the other half to Henley). In an account of Stratford in 1770 Joseph Greene said that 'about 30 years ago there was a Sunday meeting of the people called Quakers held in the town; but they have now wholly quitted it'. Why Stratford was not in an MM in our area is not clear – e.g. Alcester, further to the north, was. Friends do not seem to have flourished in Stratford until this century when they provided their own meeting house (Warwickshire MM).

(13) **Evesham** ('Evesholme')

Evesham MM 1668-1810
Worcestershire MM 1810-1859
Worcs & Shropshire MM 1859-1986
Banbury & Evesham MM since 1986

Worcestershire QM 1668-1790
Hereford & Worcs QM 1790-1832
Hereford, Worcs & Wales GM/QM 1832/1868
Western QM 1868-1966

Meeting house with warden's cottage and another cottage. Cowl Street (OS grid ref: SP 038 438).

See pages 27 and 40 for sufferings.

See page 58 for distraints.

See page 70 for attendance at meetings.

See pages 87 and 94 for adult school and mission work.

First report of a meeting was in 1656 at the house of Thomas Cartwright, probably in Port Street, Bengeworth ('Bengard').

Later Friends met at the house of Edward Pitway in Waterside, Bengeworth. The Northwick Arms Hotel is now on the site and the former burial ground (bought 1675) is in the garden of the hotel.

The present site in Cowl Street was purchased in 1676. A meeting house was built that year but it must have been flimsy as it had to be extensively rebuilt (in brick) in 1698. A burial ground was provided in 1721.

The meeting room dates from 1698 and has two unusual features. The stand was very large and had two rows of seats each with a vertical panel in front; and there was a further row of seats in front of that. The seating capacity on the two main rows of seats must have been up to 30, even without the third (front) row. The second unusual feature is in the old oak wainscoting. A number of names are scratched on it, with various dates from 1698 (when the meeting house was rebuilt) until 1712. It is thought that the meeting house was used as a school in its early days as the names scratched on it are those of young Friends who were adults there a few years later. We know from the records that a school was running there in 1713; but know no more about it.

For much of the 18th century Evesham MM consisted of only two meetings – Evesham and Alcester. Indeed, it sometimes called itself 'Evesham and Alcester MM'. In the minutes a distinction is made between the two – Evesham Friends were 'present' and those from Alcester were shown separately as 'by appointment'.

In 1823 a cottage was bought (which now houses the Citizens Advice Bureau) and in 1838 the room over the porch was enlarged. In 1874 the Warden's house was improved, and other work on the meeting house was carried out in 1870 and 1892. In the 1980s the meeting room was in a poor state and was substantially refurbished by members of the meeting (in the course of which the outer vertical panel of the stand was removed). For the Cowl Street Hall see Chapter 5.

The meeting house remains in use (with Wardens) but the burial ground is closed.

(14) **Hook Norton** ('Hookingnorton')

Banbury MM 1668-1932 (but several periods in 19th century when closed).
Oxfordshire QM 1668-1790
Berks & Oxon QM 1790-1932

Southrop, Hook Norton (OS grid ref: SP 358 328).

First report of a meeting there 1668.

The meeting house was built (no burial ground) in 1705; it was the first non-conformist building in Hook Norton. (There are suggestions that there was an earlier meeting elsewhere in the town, but there is no confirmation.)

In 1781, it was decided that Hook Norton and South Newington should have a joint PM and meet at alternate places. In 1810 it came under Sibford for PM purposes. By 1834 it had its own PM again; until 1865 when it went back with Sibford.

Around about 1850 there was a local industry making poke bonnets, which were then fashionable, and some were 'for the many local Quaker ladies'.

In about 1883, for a few years, a meeting for worship was held in a barn in or near Hook Norton for the men constructing the Cheltenham to Banbury Railway. They were 'well attended by villagers but not many railway workers'. Sibford Meeting was also involved.

In 1888 the meeting was discontinued. Thereafter the Primitive Methodists had part use of the meeting house (and maintained it) but Friends reserved their right to use it.

From 1888 to 1932 Hook Norton opened and closed more than once. The information available is uncertain but it is thought that in 1893-1910 there was an allowed meeting (under Sibford); and there were some 'Public Meetings'. From 1914 to 1932 there was a meeting only about once in five weeks with about 20-25 present. The last marriage was in 1915, there had not been one since 1854. The couple who married became the parents of Muriel Langley, now of Banbury Meeting.

In 1932 the meeting was finally discontinued and the meeting house demolished as it was unsafe. The site was later sold and has not been built upon.

(15) **Littleton**

Worcester & Shropshire MM 1899-1986   Western QM 1899-1966
Banbury & Evesham MM since 1986

The meeting house is in Shinehill Road, South Littleton, three miles east of Evesham (OS grid ref: SP 803 462).

See pages 91 and 94 for history of the meeting.

Mission meetings were held from the early 1880s. The 'Friends' Mission Room' (always known as 'The Room') was built in 1898 in brick. It was a recognised meeting in 1899 and had its own PM from 1904. It had a small stables at one time.

It merged with Evesham in 1986 and is now a recognised meeting without a PM. There is a meeting for worship on the third

Sunday of each month and a fellowship meeting each Sunday evening.

It is still in use and in the ownership of Friends.

(16) **Long Compton** (All one word at one time)
Warwickshire South MM 1668-1831
Warwickshire QM 1668-1790
Warwickshire, Leics & Rutland QM 1790-1831

Six miles south-east of Shipston-on-Stour. What used to be the meeting house (built in local stone) is in Malthouse Lane; after it was discontinued, it was a barn for many years but was converted into a private house in 1989. The burial ground is in the garden of 'The Malthouse' next door (OS grid ref: SP 288 329).

See page 44 for sufferings.

First report of a meeting there 1661.

The meeting house was built, and the burial ground provided, in 1670. In 1689 the estimated number of those attending (of all ages) was put at over 100. In the early days Long Compton had much influence in its MM – but it declined.

The MM noted that the land purchased in 1670 was 'To be used as a burying ground and meeting place for the people called Quakers as long as they shall be permitted by the civil magistrates quietly and peacably to assemble; but if, for any reason of molestation from the civil magistrates (which God forbid), they shall be hindered from attending thereof, or burying their dead, to be then held for such use and service as the trustees shall think fit'.

In 1798 it had a joint PM with Stow and in 1831 it was discontinued having only one member. However, MM continued to meet there for some years. The building was sold by MM in 1859 but re-purchased again by QM in 1869 as they did not think it should have been sold. It was sold again by QM in 1949.

(16a) In 1731 a meeting was registered as a subsidiary meeting to Long Compton at the house of Timms Archer at **Wichford** (OS grid ref: SP 315 346). It was discontinued about 1830.

(17) **Netherton**
Dealing directly with Worcestershire QM 1668-1736
Evesham MM 1736-1803
Worcestershire QM 1736-1790
Hereford & Worcester QM 1790-1803

Near Elmley Castle five miles south-east of Evesham (OS grid ref: (village) SO 986 405).

First report of a meeting there 1666.

There is no known meeting house or burial ground. The meeting sent representatives to Worcestershire QM in its own right (it does not seem to have been called an MM) until 1736 when it became part of Evesham MM. By 1760 it had only one meeting a month. The meeting was discontinued in 1803.

(18) **North Newington** ('North Newton')

Banbury MM 1668-1698   Oxfordshire QM same dates.

Two and a half miles south-west of Banbury (OS grid ref: (village) SP 420 399).

First record of a meeting there 1666.

No meeting house or burial ground. Friends first met at the house of Nathanael Ball.

George Fox was there in 1668. 'We settled the monthly meetings in the power of the Lord and Friends were very glad of them'.

Nathanael Ball was a leading Quaker but was disgraced. In 1698 a document was signed by various Friends about 'The scandalous behaviour of Nathanael Ball at Oxford . . . we find that for truth's sake we cannot but take some course according to the good order of truth . . .' A report of a visit to him said 'Having thoroughly and in much love discoursed with him in relation to matters in which he hath caused truth to suffer; and he having had full time to disclose his mind; it is our advice to him that he forbear appearing at our Monthly or Quarterly Meetings as a member, or public meetings as a ministering Friend, and that he do take care, for the clearance of truth of that reproach which hath brought upon it by him; and that for the further satisfaction of Friends he should consent to the removal of the meeting from his house'. Later Nathanael Ball acknowledged that he had been guilty of drinking 'through keeping company' and was disowned.

After 1698 there was probably no meeting in the village, Friends going to Banbury. Later, in 1731, the house of one Fardon (maybe a clock maker) was registered for meetings; but there is no other information. In the 17th century there were said to be about 12 Quaker families in the village but by 1820 there was only one family there.

Friends owned an 'estate' at North Newington which produced an income for the MM for many years which was used, mostly, for helping poor Friends. It was disposed of late in the 19th century.

(19) **Pershore**

Dealing directly with Worcestershire QM 1668-1699 (or was 'Pershore MM')
Evesham MM 1699-1803
Worcestershire QM 1668-1790
Hereford & Worcester QM 1790-1803

The meeting house was in a garden behind No. 51 Bridge Street. It is not known when it was provided and it no longer exists (OS grid ref: SO 952 454). The burial ground is thought to have been at the corner of High Street and Head Street; a burial ground was found there in 1973, when the premises of the Central Garage were being extended.

First record of a meeting there was in 1662 (see page 42).

From 1668 to 1699 (when it was transferred to Evesham MM) Pershore dealt direct with Worcestershire QM but it has also been described as 'Pershore MM'; but as far as is known, there was no other meeting involved with Pershore.

In 1719 meetings were held only once a month; in 1742 once a quarter; and by 1796 once a year. In 1799 the meeting house was thoroughly repaired but, despite this, the end came in 1803 when the meeting was discontinued. In 1801 the burial ground ('now turned into a garden ground') was leased out and in 1813 the meeting house was sold.

(20) **Radway**

Shipston MM 1668-1790
Warwickshire South MM 1790-1851

Warwickshire QM 1668-1790
Warks, Leics & Rutland QM 1790-1851

Nine miles north-west of Banbury at the foot of Edge Hill. The meeting house is now a private house called 'Oriel Cottage' opposite the Recreation Ground. There was a burial ground there but there is no trace of it now. A wing has been added to the house and all of it is still thatched (OS grid ref: SP 372 483).

See page 45 for sufferings.

First record of a meeting there was in 1659 when Thomas Palmer and Richard Mills had two mares taken from them in lieu of tithes. In 1661 the meeting was broken up by armed men.

In 1665 Robert Hyarne was presented for having a meeting in his house and again in 1669 when it was said there were about 30 at the meeting. In 1689 a meeting was registered in the name of Walter Hythornes (probably the same family name as Robert Hyarne, spelling was erratic in those days) and it was said that there were over 100 Quakers in the district.

The meeting house was built and a burial ground provided in 1702. In 1703 a meeting house was registered in the name of William Hunt – probably the same building.

By 1841 the meeting was very small and Ettington took over as PM. There was a marriage there in 1845. In 1851 the meeting was discontinued as there was only one Quaker left. In 1854 John Enoch of Sibford bought the property for relatives – it was in a very dilapidated state. It was a condition that Friends could buy it back if they wished; for some reason QM considered this in 1900 but did not take any action.

(20a)   In 1735 a subsidiary meeting was in **Middle Tysoe** in the house of Richard Mallins (OS grid ref: (village) SP 342 443). No more is known of it.

(21)   **Redditch** ('Red Ditch')

Redditch MM 1668-1706   Worcestershire QM 1668-1766
Evesham MM 1706-1766

(An entirely new Redditch Meeting came into existence in 1937; it is in Warwickshire MM)

It is not known when Friends first met at Redditch but presumably they had a meeting by 1660 when Alcester (a part of Redditch MM) was known to be settled.

In 1708 a meeting house and burial ground were provided but there is no information on their whereabouts (OS grid ref: (town) SP 045 675).

The MM was transferred to Evesham MM 1706. By 1761 Redditch Friends only met 'rarely' and, by 1771, only once a year. The meeting was discontinued in 1766 and the property was sold in 1820.

Little is known of Redditch MM but, in addition to Redditch PM and Alcester, it seems to have consisted (until 1706 when all went to Evesham MM) of the small and short-lived meetings mentioned below. It has been suggested that Bishampton and Norton Beauchamp were one and the same, or that the meeting started in Bishampton and transferred to Norton Beauchamp, but the position is uncertain.

(21a) **Ridgeway** ('Rudgeway'). George Fox was there in 1677 with William Dewsbury; he had just visited Viscountess Conway at nearby Ragley Hall. They stayed in the house of John Stanley and it is thought that the meeting dates from then.

The Ridgeway runs north/south from Redditch to Astwood Bank and Alcester; John Stanley lived at Cladswell a little to the west of the A441 at the south end of the ridge (OS grid ref: (village) SP 052 588) and it is thought that Friends met in his house.

John Stanley I died in 1706 and his son, John Stanley II, seems to have continued the meeting in the house; he had crops distrained almost every year 1741-1775. The meeting was discontinued in 1737 and the members transferred to Alcester. John Stanley II gave Friends a plot of land at Cladswell for a burial ground. This is probably the burial ground at Cladswell which Alcester Friends used from the 18th century until some time in the 19th century (item (2) above).

(21b) **Bishampton** is eight miles north-west of Evesham (OS grid ref: (village) SO 990 518). A meeting was started there not later than 1701 in the house of Richard Kinman. There is no record of a meeting house or burial ground or when the meeting was discontinued.

(21c) **Norton Beauchamp** ('Nanton' or 'Norton') is 10 miles north-west of Evesham. The meeting was registered in 1729 when it must have been part of Evesham MM. There was a meeting house which was sold when the meeting was discontinued in 1748. There is no information about its whereabouts in the village (OS grid ref: (village) SO 964 524).

(21d) **Kington** ('Kineton', 'Laights Green' or 'Lights Green') is 12 miles north-west of Evesham (OS grid ref: (village) SO 990 558). The first record of a meeting there was in 1690 when Richard Laight had a distraint issued against him for non-payment of tithes; and the meeting was probably in his house. On his death in 1724 he left a 'little tenement' to Friends. The meeting was probably discontinued in 1748 when the property was sold. There is no information as to its whereabouts.

Note: Redditch Meeting was re-created in 1937 when an allowed meeting was set up. But it was not in Worcestershire and Shropshire MM as one might have expected (Redditch was always in Worcestershire) but in Warwickshire MM. The reason for this is not clear but it may be because, in 1936, Warwick, Leicester and Stafford QM together with Western QM agreed to the setting up of Warwickshire MM. The two QMs were concerned about distances between meetings and it may be that they thought that Redditch, which is close to the Warwickshire border and had good communications to Birmingham, would be best placed in Warwickshire MM. Later Redditch acquired a meeting house and is now a flourishing meeting – but it is in Warwickshire MM and not now in our area.

(22) **Shipston** (on Stour) ('Shipstone')
Shipston MM 1668-1790 (Sometimes called 'Stour MM')
Warwickshire South MM 1790-1936
Warwickshire MM 1936-1956
Warwickshire QM 1668-1790
Warks, Leics & Rutland QM 1790-1854
Warks, Leics & Staffs QM 1854-1956

See page 45 for sufferings.

See page 55 for decline of Warwickshire South MM.

See page 95 for adult school and mission work.

First report of a meeting there was in 1655 – it is said to have been started by William Parre.

By 1662 the number of Friends was put at 28 and, by 1682, 78 (not counting children in either year). The meeting house was provided in 1685 together with a burial ground. It was converted from a cottage leased from the Dean and Chapter of Worcester Cathedral; in 1875 it was purchased from them. It has been reported that, at one time, there was a passage under the south end of what is now the meeting house. 'This had, at some time, been closed by a wall and a window, and a door broken into it from the adjoining house, the tenants of which used it as a room – which considerably added to the risk of damage by fire.'

In 1689 three houses in Shipston were registered as having Quaker Meetings. The first was the meeting house (in Mill Street (OS grid ref: SP 259 406)) and the second a cottage in Mill Street. The third was Falstaff House, 33 Sheep Street, having a plaque dated 1683 with the initial 'W.V' The initials stood for William Waring and his wife Victoria who were Quakers. The plaque (in old spelling) reads 'Here we pray for peace in our land and we success with this in hand'.

In 1956 Shipston Meeting was discontinued. Shipston Meeting House is still owned by Friends and is leased to Warwickshire County Council for the local library. The disused burial ground is also still owned by Friends.

(22a) **Blackwell** is three-quarters of a mile west of the A429 near Tredington and a mile south of Armscote. The hall (see below) is the last house on the left leaving Blackwell on the more easterly of the two roads running south from the village (OS grid ref: SP 243 433).

A cottage was bought by W. B. Gibbins, of Ettington Meeting, in about 1902. He had it pulled down and built a hall in its place. Shipston Friends used it for mission meetings, twice on Sundays and for the most part for old people, until about 1919. An allowed meeting was held there from 1916 until 1919. In 1917 a Sunday school for children was being run in the village – not in the hall – and it is thought to have gone on until about 1923.

(23) **Shutford** ('Shetford')   Warwickshire QM 1668-1790
Banbury MM 1668-1804   Berks & Oxon QM 1790-1804

Shutford is five miles west of Banbury. The meeting house is now a private dwelling – 'Quaker Cottage' in Ivy Lane. (OS grid ref: SP 386 404).

First report of a meeting there 1668.

The meeting house was built and burial ground provided in 1689. The burial ground is now the garden of the house and a few gravestones remain. Inside the house there is reported to be an oak staircase (probably original) and the remains of two lofts, each with shutters. The building was thatched but now has a tile roof.

There were said to be 17 Quaker family names at Shutford in the 17th century, 23 in the 18th and five in the 19th. In 1779 MM met at South Newington, instead of Shutford, because of the smallpox at the latter. In 1786, Shutford and Banbury merged for PM purposes; they met at each place alternately but later only at Banbury.

In 1804 the meeting was discontinued. The burial ground remained in use until 1851.

In 1814 the meeting house was let, subject to Friends having the right to hold meetings there. In 1823 a meeting was held at Shutford – an unusual event it seems. In 1830 local Friends agreed to convert the meeting house into two cottages in such a way that the whole of the building could be used for having a meeting there. Both cottages were let. In 1860 there were repairs to the building and the sinking of a well. In 1880 the meeting house was sold.

(24) **Sibford** ('Sibbard')

Banbury MM 1668-1986 Oxfordshire QM 1668-1790
Banbury & Evesham MM Berks & Oxon QM 1790-1966
since 1986

See page 79 for Sibford School.

See page 97 for adult school and mission work.

The first report of a meeting was in 1668, probably at the house of Thomas Gilkes, a pioneering clockmaker.

George Fox was there in 1670 and again in 1678. On the later occasion, he stayed with Joseph Harris (the house is said to be 'Holly House' at Sibford Ferris where the Headmaster of Sibford School now lives); Fox had a meeting in a barn 'whereunto there resorted many hundreds of people'.

The first meeting house was built (and a burial ground provided) in 1678-81. It was a stone-floored building with a stone roof and stood where the paving stones, in front of the present meeting house, are now; it faced east-west. It had a lobby entrance and a loft was built over this in 1736 (facing the stand) which could be enclosed by shutters so that men and women could have separate business meetings. In 1706 the burial ground was enlarged.

In 1808 a Quaker school was set up in Sibford Ferris (or possibly Burdrop) but nothing else is known about it. It had no connection with the present school at Sibford Ferris.

In 1864 the present meeting house was built (in local stone) and was opened the following year at Sibford General Meeting (i.e. for Sibford School). It was built partly on the site of the former meeting house and partly on land given by John Soden. It had at one time been proposed that the cost would be met by the sale of meeting house properties at Shutford and South Newington, but this idea was dropped and the necessary funds were found. The reason for building a new meeting house was that the old one had, since Sibford School opened in 1842, become too small.

Originally the new meeting room was divided in the middle of the room by a large wooden partition, the lower portion of which was at about the height of the seats (with a door through) and, between the top of this and the ceiling, were two cumbrous shutters which moved up and down like sash windows. This was to allow separate business meetings for men and women. However, the shutters were removed in 1891 when heating was put in and men had their business meeting in the meeting room and women in the (new) mission room. Wood from the old partitions was used for wainscoting in the mission room.

In 1879 three cottages adjoining the meeting house were purchased. They had previously opened into a courtyard roughly where the entrance gates (built at that time) are today. New walls and paths (and a well) were provided and the first cottage was for a caretaker. The two remaining cottages were converted into a mission room and other facilities (see Chapter 5).

For a few years from 1883 Sibford and Hook Norton had a meeting for railway construction workers – see Hook Norton (item 14 of this appendix).

The meeting house remains in use. The burial ground is also open – the only one in Banbury and Evesham MM.

(25) **South Newington** ('South Newton')
Banbury MM 1668-1825 and 1892-1911
Oxfordshire QM 1668-1790
Berks & Oxon QM 1790-1825 and 1892-1911

Six miles south-west of Banbury. The meeting house, built in local stone, is now the Village Hall in St. Peter's Close. (OS grid ref: SP 406 331). The burial ground is in the garden.

See item (1) of this appendix for 'George Fox's table'.

First report of a meeting there 1663.

The meeting house was built in 1692. It is unusual (for a meeting house) in that there is a plaque with a Latin inscription 'Domus Hec Que Edificeret Anno Domini 1692' with three sets of initials. The first was 'TB' for Timothy Burbelow of Aynho; 'RC' was Richard Claridge (who had been an Anglican clergyman before becoming a Quaker); and 'JF' was Joan French from whom the land was purchased. It is understood that the original loft is still there. A porch (and perhaps an outbuilding at the side) was built in 1927 after Friends had sold it.

South Newington is said to have had 8 Quakers in 1663 and 30 in 1676 of which 'a large number were freeholders'. In 1781 the PMs of Hook Norton and South Newington merged – meeting alternately. In 1802 South Newington came under Banbury for PM purposes and in 1814 under Sibford. In 1816-17 the possibility of closure was discussed. It would seem that part of the meeting house was let out at that time.

In 1825 the meeting was discontinued and the remaining Friends were transferred to Hook Norton. After this date, the building was used by Friends from time to time and also by Methodists.

In 1892 there was an MM discussion on the future of the meeting house, which was in a poor state of repair. The village was thought to be declining – so what was the future of the meeting? However, a proposal to sell it was not accepted. Charles Gillett and Wilks Brown proposed to repair the meeting house at their own cost on the understanding that they could use it for temperance and mission meetings. This was accepted and the meeting house re-opened for these purposes in 1892. There was a meeting for worship once a fortnight. It had no PM and came under Banbury.

The meeting was discontinued in 1911 and the building sold in 1927.

(26) **Stow** (on the Wold)

Campden & Stow MM 1668-1790　Gloucestershire QM 1668-1785
Warwickshire South MM　　　　Glos & Wilts QM 1785-1790
1790-1852　　　　　　　　　　Warks, Leics & Rutland QM
　　　　　　　　　　　　　　　1790-1852

The site of the former meeting house is behind the Old Stocks Hotel (formerly the Red Lion) in The Square. (OS grid ref: SP 193 258). The meeting house has been converted into a private house (owned by the hotel) and the burial ground is under the hotel car park. A plaque was erected in 1988, by the Stow Society and Banbury and Evesham MM, to mark the site.

Friends are said to have first met there in 1668.

Land for the meeting house was purchased in 1719 and the meeting house (and stables) were finished by 1724. The burial ground may have been used before that date. There were two Quaker families at Lower Swell in 1683 but only one a 100 years later; and there was a Quaker family at Broadwell in 1735. These Friends would have belonged to Stow Meeting.

Stow was always a small meeting. In 1735 there were said to be 15 Quakers there and only two in 1750; but this may refer to families. Stow joined with other nearby meetings for PM purposes; with Long Compton in 1798 and with Shipston in 1841. In 1851 there was said to be only one Quaker family able to get to Stow Meeting, but they went to Chipping Norton Meeting (outside our area).

In 1852 the meeting was discontinued. The building was sold in 1886 and the money used to repair Shipston Meeting House. The burial ground was not sold until 1965.

(26a) A meeting associated with Stow was registered at **Oddington** (OS grid ref: (village) SP 229 259) in 1707 at the house of Richard Haydon. In 1750 there were two Quaker families there, one of whom lost goods by distraint on several occasions. No more is known.

APPENDIX 2

How Friends Earned Their Living

GIVEN BELOW IS AN ANALYSIS of the employments of Friends taken from the summaries of marriage records of Banbury MM. No occupations were given in about 15% of the entries. Occupations given for women are ignored; two were housemaids in the earliest period and all others were 'spinster' or 'widow'. Most entries were for the period 1700-1749 and numbers fall away thereafter. The number of Quaker marriages may have been falling or the summaries may not be complete.

Occupation	Nos to 1699	Nos 1700-1749	Nos 1750-1799	Nos 1800-1850
Farmer	–	–	1	6
Yeoman	11	25	9	1
Husbandman	8	17	1	–
Gardener	2	1	–	–
Grazier	–	4	–	–
Shepherd	–	1	–	–
Maltster	1	7	4	1
Miller	1	6	2	–
Mealman	–	–	1	–
Flax dresser	–	3	1	–
Hemp dresser	–	–	2	1
Hosier	–	–	–	1
Weaver (various)	2	7	4	–
Tailor	2	5	–	–
Draper (various)	4	2	1	–
Haberdasher of hats	1	–	–	–
Glover	–	1	1	1
Lace maker	–	1	–	–
Clothier	–	–	1	–

HOW FRIENDS EARNED THEIR LIVING

Cont.

Occupation	Nos to 1699	Nos 1700-1749	Nos 1750-1799	Nos 1800-1850
Shoemaker or Cordwainer	3	18	10	–
Fuller	1	2	–	–
Threadmaker	–	1	–	–
Woolstapler	–	–	1	–
Barber and periwig maker	–	1	–	–
Mercer	2	11	1	–
Blacksmith	4	5	3	–
Cooper	–	1	–	–
Ironmonger	–	1	–	–
Locksmith	2	–	–	–
Turner	1	1	–	–
Pewterer	1	–	–	–
Wheelwright	1	3	–	2
Tanner	–	1	–	–
Carpenter	3	6	2	2
Timber merchant	–	–	–	1
Mason	–	1	–	–
Joiner	1	1	–	–
Stone cutter	–	1	–	–
Butcher	–	1	1	1
Baker	1	7	7	3
Grocer	1	1	2	2
Merchant	–	1	–	–
Tallow chandler	2	–	–	–
Cutler	1	–	–	–
Clock and/or watchmaker	–	3	3	5
Carrier	2	1	–	–
Distiller	–	1	–	–
Papermaker	–	1	–	–
Druggist/apothecary	–	2	–	2
Dr. of physic	1	–	–	–
Schoolmaster	2	1	1	–
Law-man	–	1	–	–
Servant	2	–	–	–
Labourer	5	2	–	–
TOTALS	**68**	**156**	**59**	**29**

This is, of course, an analysis for Banbury MM only – and may not be complete. The descriptions were, presumably, those given by the individuals getting married.

Summaries of marriage registers for other parts of our area are either non-existent or patchy with many occupational entries left blank. Other occupations which crop up in minutes, etc. elsewhere in our area include:

> Gent
> Tobacconist
> Solicitor
> Barber-surgeon
> Shopkeeper
> Dealer in clothes
> Woolcomber
> Milliner

APPENDIX 3

Bibliography and Notes on Sources

Published Books

Balfour, Hugh, *The Quakers in Puritan England*, Yale, 1963.

Barrett, Philip, *The Book of Pershore*, Barracuda Books, Buckingham, 1980.

Beesley, Alfred, *A History of Banbury*, Nichols & Son, London, 1841.

Beeson, C. F. C., *Quaker Clockmakers*, The Antique Collector, October 1958.

Besse, Joseph, *A Collection of the Sufferings of the People called Quakers*, London, 1753 (and other dates).

Braithwaite, William Charles, *The Beginnings of Quakerism* and *The Second Period of Quakerism*, Sessions, 1981 and 1979.

Braithwaite, J. Bevan, *A Friend in the 19th century*, Hodder and Stoughton, 1909.

Brown, Alfred W., *Evesham Friends in the Olden Time*, West, Newman & Co., London, 1885.

Butler, David, *Friends Sufferings 1650-1688: a Comparative Study*, Journal of the Friends Historical Society, Vol. 55, No. 6.

Carter, Charles, *Unsettled Friends*, Journal of the Friends Historical Society, 1967.

Christian Faith and Practice in the Experience of the Society of Friends. Published by Friends House, London from time to time.

Coleman, C. D., *The Economy of England 1450-1750*, Oxford University Press, 1977.

Darlington, C. D., *The Evolution of Man and Society*, George Allen and Unwin, 1969.

Fox, George, *Journal*, edited by John L. Nickalls, Cambridge, 1952.
Friendly Mission, *The Missionary Enterprises at Evesham*, August 1907.
Gorman, Mark, *Broad Campden Quakers*, Friends Home Service, 1971.
Greenwood, J. Ormerod, *Quaker Encounters* (three separate volumes), Sessions, 1977.
Hill, Christopher, *The World Turned Upside Down*, Penguin, 1975 (and a number of other fine books on the 17th century).
Hutton, Ronald, *The Restoration*, Oxford, 1985.
Jones, Rufus M., *The Later Periods of Quakerism*, Macmillan, 1921.
Lester, Marjorie, *Memories of Banbury*, Lester, 1986.
Lidbetter, Hubert, *The Friends Meeting House*, Sessions, 1979.
Newman, George, *Quaker Profiles*, Bannisdale Press, 1946.
Nicholson, Marjorie H., *Conway Letters*, Oxford, 1920.
Noakes, John, *Worcestershire Sects*, Longman, 1861.
Penney, Norman, *The First Publishers of Truth*, Headley Bros., 1907.
Pickvance, Joseph, *A Reader's Companion to George Fox's Journal*, Quaker Home Service, 1989.
Punshon, John, *Portrait in Grey*, Quaker Home Service, 1984.
Raistrick, Arthur, *Quakers in Science and Industry*, David & Charles, 1950.
Reay, Barry, *Quakers in the English Revolution*, St. Martins Press, New York, 1985.
Ross, Isabel, *Margaret Fell: Mother of Quakerism*, Longman Green, 1949.
Rowntree, J. Wilhelm and Binns, Henry (with introduction by Christopher Charlton), *A History of the Adult School Movement*, University of Nottingham, 1983.
Southall, Kenneth H., *Our Quaker Heritage: early Quaker Meeting Houses*, Friends Home Service Committee.
Smith, Richard H., *Quakerism in the Vale of Evesham*, The Wayfarer, October and November, 1933.
Stevens, S. H., *Anne, Viscountess Conway*, Friends Quarterly Examiner, 1874.
Sturge, C. D. and others, *An Account of the Charitable Trusts and other Properties Belonging to Friends in Warwickshire, Leicestershire and Stafford QM*, White & Pike, Birmingham, 1891.
Taylor, Audrey M., *Gilletts, Bankers of Banbury and Oxford*, Clarendon, 1964.

BIBLIOGRAPHY AND NOTES ON SOURCES

Taylor, Ernest E., *The Valiant Sixty*, Sessions, 1988.
Trevelyan, G. M., *British History in the 19th Century*, Longman Green, 1924.
Trinder, Barry, *Victorian Banbury*, Banbury Historical Society, 1982.
Trinder, Barry, *The Origins of Quakerism in Banbury*, Journal of the Banbury Historical Society, 1979.
Victorian History of England (The) (by counties).
Watts, Michael, *The Dissenters*, Clarendon, 1978.
WEA History Workshop, *Crime in the Vale of Evesham 1651-70*, Hereford and Worcester County Libraries, 1987.
White, William, *Friends in Warwickshire in the 17th and 18th centuries*, White & Pike, Birmingham, 1873.
Workers at Home and Abroad, Pioneering in Rural England, *The Story of Quakerism in Littleton*, January and February 1916.

Unpublished sources

Lamb, Joshua (1856-1943), 'Recollections of Sibford Meeting'. In the ownership of Ina and Arnold Lamb of Sibford Ferris; extracts are reproduced with their permission.

Location of QM, MM, PM minutes and allied papers relating to our area – to the extent that they still exist

Banbury MM and its PMs Banbury & Evesham MM and its PMs [intention is all will eventually be at Oxford]	County Record Office, Oxford.
Oxfordshire QM Berks & Oxon QM	Berkshire County Record Office, Reading.
Shipston MM and its PMs Warwickshire South MM and its PMs Campden & Stow MM and its PMs Warwickshire MM Warwickshire QM Warwickshire, Leicester & Rutland QM Warwickshire, Leicester & Stafford QM	Archives of Warwickshire MM at Bull St. Birmingham. Photocopies of these, with other documents of interest, at County Record Office, Warwick. Some early records (QM mostly) about Shipston and Armscote at the Hereford & Worcester County Record Office at Worcester.

Campden/Broad Campden PM Stow PM	Most papers at Bull St. (as above) but some of interest at County Record Office, Gloucester.
Gloucester MM and its PMs Gloucester & Nailsworth MM and its PMs Gloucestershire QM Glos & Wilts QM	County Record Office, Gloucester.
Evesham MM and its PMs together with (rather shadowy) information about MMs/Meetings at Broadway, Pershore, Redditch & Netherton Worcestershire MM and its PMs Worcester & Shropshire MM and its PMs Worcestershire QM Hereford & Worcester QM Hereford, Worcester & Wales GM/QM Western QM	Hereford & Worcester County Record Office at Worcester.
Friends House Library Euston Road, London NW1 2BJ	Holds a great deal of information – well documented.

Selected Index

Only QM and MM references of particular interest are included. The names of many individuals (particularly those who only appear once in the text) have not been included.

ABJURATION, Act of, 21, 22, 26, 28
Ackworth School, 104, 109
Adderbury, 15, 22, 34, 49, 56, 65, 67, 69, 70, 102, 117-19
Adult schools – see schools
Adult schools, Nat Council of, 86
Alcester, 33, 34, 49, 51, 58, 119-21
Allegiance, Oath of – see praemunire
Allen, William, 84
America(ns), 7, 50, 55, 56, 74, 77, 85, 106, 112, 125
Anabaptists, 18, 35
Anglican Church/Anglicans, 22, 27, 36, 37, 44, 54, 76
Apprenticeship, 19, 104
Armscote, 14, 34, 45, 46, 49, 69, 70-74, 96, 121
Ash, George & Maria, 87, 89, 91, 95
Ashbee, Mr & Mrs C. R., 77
Associate membership, 96, 97
Audland, John & Ann, 19, 25-27
Australia, 55, 66

BADSEY, 8, 69, 87-95, 121-2
Ball, Nathanael, 25, 132
Banbury (inc. Neithrop), 9, 15, 25-27, 31, 34, 39, 40, 49, 50, 55, 57, 58, 69, 84, 98-102, 105, 114, 122-3
Banbury MM, 9, 56, 64, 97, 142
Banbury & Evesham MM, 9, 59, 140
Banbury & Sibford Friends Tract & Library Assoc., 97

Band of Hope – see Temperance
Banking & Bankers, 57, 64, 99, 104
Baptists (particular & other), 18, 34, 76
Barclay, Robert, 51
Barton, 49, 123
Bayliss (family name), 42, 65, 95
Beezley, Samuel, 57, 99
Bengeworth, 28, 128
Berks & Oxon QM, 73, 79
Berry, Major General, 30
Besse, Joseph, 24, 25, 46, 145
Be(a)vingtons (family name), 56, 63, 64, 75, 114
Bicester, 49, 124
Bishampton, 135
Blackwell, 96, 137
Blasphemy (including Act of), 21, 26
Blockley, 55, 75, 76, 78, 125
Bloxham, 49, 56, 119
Bracey, Bertha, 106
Brailes, 33, 34, 49, 55, 57, 65, 76, 125
Braithwaites (family name), 45, 68, 99, 112, 145
Brass Bands, 92, 93, 102
Breda, Declaration of, 23
Bristol Yearly Meeting, 14, 110, 111
British Schools, 84, 88, 99
British & Foreign Schools Society, 84
Broad Campden, 9, 11, 15, 32-34, 43, 49, 55, 56, 64, 65, 69, 74-80, 112

149

Broadway (& 'Broadway MM'), 33,
   34, 42, 46, 49, 58, 87, 126
Broughton, 26, 30, 49, 123
Brown, Alfred W. & William W., 7, 8,
   87, 89, 145
Brown, Lizzie & Lottie, 7, 99
Brummana, 112
Bubb, Frederick & Thomas, 95
Buck, Sophie Fanny, 118
Burlington, Henry, 89
Butler, David, 46

CADBURYS (family name), 57, 93, 98, 99
Camm, John & Mabel, 25, 26, 31
Campden – see Broad Campden
Campden & District Historical & Archaeological Society, 9
Campden & Stow MM, 55, 75
Cartwright, Thomas, 28, 29, 31, 128
Catholics, Roman (inc. Papists), 21, 23, 25, 28, 38, 91
Certificate of Pre-vocational Education, 81
Cherwell, 99-101
Chipping Campden – see Broad Campden
Chipping Norton, 57, 141
Christian Endeavour, 88-102
Church
  – Rates, 16, 19, 20, 27, 31, 38, 58, 61, 107, 108, 109
  – Speaking in, 21, 22, 25, 31, 32, 36, 40
  – Non attendance at, 22, 37, 43, 44, 45
Circular Meetings, 8, 14, 110, 111
Cirencester, 78
Cladswell – see Ridgeway
Clarendon, Lord, 40
Classes – see Schools
Clockmaking, 7, 56, 104, 118
Commons, House of – see Parliament
Concerts, 86, 93, 94

Conventicle
  – Acts of, 36, 37
  – meetings at, 29, 32, 33, 36, 39, 40, 42, 43, 44, 45, 134
Conway, Viscountess, 50, 51, 120, 135
Corks (family name), 65, 75
'Creaturely activities', 97
Cromwell, Richard & Oliver, 21, 23, 28, 29, 31
Culworth, 27

DARLINGTON, Prof. C. D., 53, 145
Davidson, Asher, 95
Deddington, 56
Dewsbury, William, 135
Disownments, 16, 55, 62, 64, 67, 79, 105, 132
Distraints, 24, 27, 31, 38, 40, 43, 44, 56, 58, 59, 61, 134, 135, 141
D'Oyly, Bray, 25, 70, 82, 117
D'Oyly, Bray, Housing Assoc., 82, 83

EAST HOUSE, 81, 82
Edge Hill, 34
Education Acts, 86
Ettington, 9, 15, 34, 43, 49, 56, 60, 63, 69, 74, 96, 114, 127
Evangelical movement, 76, 83, 84, 99
Evans, William & Joan, 50
Evesham, 8, 9, 27-32, 34, 40-42, 49, 50, 58, 70, 73, 84, 86, 87-95, 110, 128
Evesham MM, 46, 56, 64, 65
Evesham prisons, 32
Excommunication, 22, 44, 45
Eydon, 27

FAMILISTS, 18
Fardons (family name), 7, 56, 132
Farnsworth, Richard, 26, 27
Fell, Margaret & Rachel, 35, 36, 70
Fellowship meetings – see mission meetings
Fiennes – see Saye & Sele, Lord
Fifth Monarchy Men, 18, 24, 35, 36
Field, Robert, 24, 44

SELECTED INDEX

'Flower de Luce', 27
Fox, George, 9, 18, 19, 29, 31, 34, 35, 42, 46, 51, 53, 70, 118, 132, 135, 138, 146
Fox, George's table, 118
Fox, Margaret, 70
Friends First Day School Assoc., 86
Friends Foreign Mission Assoc., 106
Friends Home Mission Committee, 87, 88, 89
Friends Relief Service, 102

GIBBINS (family name), 63, 64, 73, 74, 96, 137
Gilkes (family name), 56, 75, 138
Gilletts (family name), 54, 57, 58, 66, 75, 76, 99, 112, 140
Gloucester & Nailsworth MM, 77, 78
Gloucester(shire), 9, 33, 46, 68, 87, 110
Gloucestershire QM, 75, 107
Goodaire, Thomas, 27, 43
'Gooseberry Sunday', 73
Gospel meetings – see mission meetings
Greenwood, J. Ormerod, 10, 84, 146
Grimsbury, 99, 100, 101
Gurney, Joseph John, 57, 79

HAINE, Frank & Jean, 125
Halford, John, 70
Harris, Abraham & Katherine, 96
Harvest festivals, 90, 93
Hats (problems with), 20, 21, 26, 28, 29
Heyford, Lower, 50, 124
Hitchman, John & Prudence, 74, 75
Hook Norton, 40, 49, 70, 102, 115, 129
Hubberthorne, Richard, 119
Hull, Jonathan, 76

INDULGENCE, Declaration of, 37
Informers, 37, 43, 44

JEPHCOTTS (Jeffcuts) (family name), 66, 75, 118

Jones, Rufus M., 24, 146

KEYTES (Keites) (Kites) (family name), 32, 33, 75
Kidd, Benjamin, 114, 122
King
 – Charles II, 23, 24, 35-38, 45
 – George V, 78
 – James II, 38
 – William III (of Orange) & Queen Mary, 38
King's Council, 39
King, Gregory, 16
Kington, 49, 58, 135

LAMBS (family name), 7, 48, 63, 67, 97, 103, 115, 147
Lamb's War, 19
Lamley, Sarah, 111
Lancaster, Joseph, 84
Langley, Muriel, 123, 130
Lawson, Christopher, 96, 121
Levellers, 18, 21
Lidbetter, Hubert, 15, 146
Littleton, 8, 9, 70, 85, 87-95, 130
Loft, 15, 75, 117, 122
Lollards, 18
Long Compton, 34, 44, 49, 114, 131
Lord's Day Act, 22
Lords, House of – see Parliament
Lower, Thomas & Mary, 70
Lucas, Samuel, 44, 127

MAIDENWELL, 75, 77, 78
Manchester Conference, 83
Marriages, 63, 64
Marrying-out (see Disownments)
Martin, Robert, 28, 32
Marvell, Andrew, 37
McColm, Mary B., 11
Meetings deemed illegal – see Conventicles
Meeting houses – building, 39, 40, 49, 72, 74

Meetings
- for church affairs, 8, 13, 15, 16, 48, 75, 108, 118
- setting up, 27, 39, 42, 46, 49, 50, 70, 132
- in the street (see preaching)
Meetings broken up – see Conventicles, meetings at
Membership, 55, 62, 67, 92, 107, 108
Mennonites, 106
Methodists (inc. primitive), 76, 121, 130, 140
Milcombe, 39, 40, 49, 119
Militia, 58
Milligan, Edward H., 7, 11
Mission meetings, 13, 57, 69, 73, 83, 85-103, 137, 140
Missionary Helpers Union, 90, 98
Money, value of, 16
Mount Laurel Meeting (USA), 50

NEITHROP – see Banbury
Netherton, 46, 49, 58, 131
Newby, Margaret, 30
Newman, George, 19, 146
Noakes, John, 36, 146
North Newington, 40, 49, 132
Norton Beauchamp, 58, 135

OATHS, refusal to swear, 20, 21, 22, 23, 28, 32, 33, 36, 40, 45
Oddington, 141
Orders in Council, 37
'Our area', 12
Oxfam, 106
Oxford(shire), 9, 46, 57, 68
Oxfordshire, Lord Lieutenant of, 39, 40
Oxfordshire QM, 51

PAPISTS see Catholics, Roman
Parliament (Lords & Commons), 24, 27, 36, 37, 38
Parsons, Richard, 43
Penington, Isaac, 51

Penn, William, 13, 38, 51, 70
Pepys, Samuel, 20
Pershore (& 'Pershore MM'), 34, 42, 46, 49, 58, 88, 133
Philadelphia, 50, 55, 75, 124
Pickvance, Joseph, 77, 146
Pitway, Edward, 28, 29, 30, 31, 32, 128
Plush weaving, 57, 104
Praemunire (Oath of Allegiance), 23, 33, 35, 37, 39, 40, 44, 45
Preaching or meeting in street, 26, 28, 29, 30, 36, 40
Presbyterians, 28, 68
Publishers of Truth, 19, 24, 25, 26, 27, 32, 119

'QUAKER' – origin of name, 20
Quaker Act, 36
Quakers, numbers of, 55, 67, 68, 69
Queries, 13, 14, 108, 113

RADWAY, 34, 45, 49, 133
Ragley Hall, 50, 51, 120, 135
Ramallah, 112
Reay, Barry, 21, 146
Redditch (& Redditch MM), 34, 46, 49, 58, 134
Retreat, The, 105
Ridgeway, 49, 51, 58, 120, 135
'Room, The', 91-94, 130
Rostrum, 89, 91
Rowntree, John Wilhelm, 87, 146

SALVATION Army, 73, 93
Saye and Sele, Lords, James & William, 26, 27, 40, 123
Schools and classes, 8, 57, 83, 85-103, 119, 123, 129, 137, 138
Scott, Peter & Richenda, 81, 82
Shipston (on Stour), 34, 45, 50, 56, 57, 58, 70, 95-97, 101, 110, 136
Shipston MM, 55, 61, 76
Shutford, 40, 50, 57, 137

SELECTED INDEX 153

Sibford Meeting/Sibford Gower, 9, 40, 47, 48, 50, 56, 69, 70, 73, 79, 97, 98, 115, 138
Sibford School/Sibford Ferris, 56, 57, 70, 79-81, 138, 139
Sibford Old Scholars Assoc., 81
Simpson, William, 25, 31, 32
Smart, Christopher, 67
Smith, Humphrey, 27, 28, 29
Smith, Richard & Mildred, 95, 141
South Newington, 34, 40, 50, 70, 102, 118, 139
Stand, 15, 72, 75, 77, 117, 120, 127, 129
Stanley, John (I & II), 135
Stratford-on-Avon, 128
Stocks, 28, 29, 30, 33
Stow (on-the-Wold), 50, 75, 76, 140
Stow Society, 140
Sufferings
- incidence of, 45, 46, 58
- Meeting for, 14, 37
- records of, 24
  (See also Blasphemy; Church rates; Church, speaking in; Church, non-attendance at; Conventicles, Meetings at; Distraints; Excommunication; Hats (problems with); Militia; Praemunire; Preaching or meeting in the street; Sunday travel; Stocks; Tithes.)
Sunday
- Schools (see Schools)
- Travel, 22, 33

TADMARTON, 26, 50, 123
Temperance, 57, 84-103, 108, 140
Test Act & other restrictions, 39, 54
Testimonies to dead, 51, 111, 113-116
Thorne, Arthur E., 95
Threshing meetings, 73, 103
Timms, Sarah, 26
Tithes, 16, 18, 20, 38, 44, 45, 54, 58, 61, 108, 134

Tithes impropriation, 16, 33, 61
Toleration Act 1689, 38
Toleration, Declaration of 1687, 38
Travelling Friends, 8, 14, 19, 109, 112
Travel to meetings, 33, 46
Tredington, 61, 96, 121
Tysoe, Middle, 134
Tyson, Charles & Madge – dedication, 77, 78, 79

UNIFORMITY, Act of, 36

VAGRANCY, (inc. Act of), 22, 32
Vivers, Edward & Richard, 25, 27, 39, 40

WAGSTAFF, James, 27, 39, 122
Warner, Edward & William, 33, 75
Watts, Michael, 68, 147
Waugh, Jane, 26, 39
Wars (& War Victim's Cttee), 106
Warwick(shire), 9, 35, 39, 43, 44, 46, 68, 110
Warwickshire MM, 77, 78, 120, 134, 136
Warwickshire North MM, 120, 128
Warwickshire Middle MM, 128
Warwickshire South MM, 55, 72, 76, 109, 112
Warwickshire QM ⎫
Warks, Leics & Rutland QM ⎬ 72, 73, 108, 113, 120, 136
Warks, Leics & Staffs QM ⎭
Wesley, John, 84
Western QM, 73, 88, 136
West Indies, 104, 105, 106
Weston, Nathanael, 25, 26
Whitehouse, George, 32
Wichford, 131
Wilde, Major, 42
Women Friends, 14, 39, 48, 49, 75, 118, 122
Woodbrooke, 83
Worcester Abbey/Cathedral, 121, 136

Worcester(shire), 9, 36, 42, 46, 68, 70, 88, 110
Worcestershire QM, 58, 72, 108, 120
Worcs & Shropshire MM, 120, 136

Workers Education Assoc., 86
Wyatt, Alice, 61

YOUNG, Edmund, 29, 30, 32